Whither SOUTH AFRICA?

Edited by
Bernard Magubane & Ibbo Mandaza

A Publication of the African Association of Political Science

Africa World Press, Inc.
P.O. Box 1892
Trenton, New Jersey 08607   (609) 695-3766

Africa World Press, Inc.
P.O. Box 1892
Trenton, N.J. 08607

First Printing 1988

Copyright © The African Association of Political Science

Cover Design by Ife Nii Owoo

Typeset by TypeHouse of Pennington, Inc.

Library of Congress Catalog Card Number: 86-73224

ISBN: 0-86543-048-9   Cloth
       0-86543-049-7   Paper

Contents

Foreword

Opening Remarks To AAPS Seminar on "Whither South Africa"
N.M. Shamuyarira

This meeting has been convened at an appropriate time. The broad masses of South Africa have firmly decided to overthrow the yoke of apartheid and minority racist rule. Their decision now appears to be irreversible. Unlike in the past, when uprisings such as Sharpeville (1960), Langa, Pondoland, Soweto (1976), etc. were quelled by police and army opening fire and killing indiscriminately and arresting and removing the leadership, in the current uprising the masses are continuing their resistance and broadening their appeal to all strata of the black population. A related factor that should be underlined is the complete political disarray in the ranks of the ruling class in South Africa. They do not have a comprehensive political plan for their survival. In fact, the ruling class is breaking up into three distinct factions that quarrel openly about the character of apartheid. The growing disagreements among the rulers, and the mounting resistance of the ruled, creates very favorable objective and subjective conditions for revolution in South Africa. However, the regime has massive economic and military power which it can unleash to destroy any organs of revolutionary change.

The title of your seminar, "Whither South Africa," is also very appropriate. We will be waiting to hear and read about your analysis of the dominant trends in South Africa as well as in the region. The events in South Africa have a direct bearing on developments in the region. If the rule of the present reactionary and fascist forces in South Africa is consolidated, all the reactionary forces and dissident/bandit groups in the region will be strengthened correspondingly. If progressive forces win power in South Africa, a major threshold will have been crossed in man's quest for freedom, and all progressive governments in the region will have been greatly strengthened. If, however, there is chaos and economic disorder in South Africa, many countries in the region will be equally, adversely affected. To put it briefly, wherever South Africa goes, the region will be propelled to follow, at least in part.

One of the issues you will discuss is the nature and character of the South African state. Excellent papers have been written by Martin Leggasick, Harold Wolpe, Joe Slovo, Ruth First, Ben Turok, and others on this topic. The papers have stated the dependent nature of the apartheid state on black labor from the bantustans and the black neighboring states on the one hand, and on foreign investment from Western Europe and America, either directly to the state or through the multinational corporations on the other hand. Again we will be waiting to read your conclusions. The apartheid state is both violent and exploitative. There is plentiful evidence for this. However, the most peculiar feature of the apartheid state is its racial character—the ruling class is a racial oligarchy that has vast privileges of education, skills, and expertise that are generally denied to the black majority. Therefore the critical question, in both the transitional stage and the future, is how the white oligarchy will fit in or be accommodated in the new social order in South Africa. The African National Congress has spelled out its position on this important question in "the Freedom Charter." It proposes a land inhabited by all citizens, irrespective of race, color, or creed, who want to live in a democratic, independent, and sovereign republic of South Africa.

We should point out that when the South African whites realize that they can no longer suppress the mobilized black majority, in the interest of retaining some or most of their power, they will endeavor to build alliances with some of the black leaderships, especially chiefs and priests. Their functions in society make them soft targets for overtures from the rulers when they want to make peace with or divide the rising broad masses. An inventory of the actual characters who could be possible collaborators, and the categories from which they could be recruited, would be useful to the liberation movements, and especially to the OAU, which has a habit of legitimizing usurpers.

The independent African countries in the region of southern Africa are all targets of South Africa's destabilization measures at the economic and military levels. At the economic level South Africa is imposing economic sanctions on its neighbors through its control of the major transport network to the seas. A study of the transportation system in the region shows heavy dependence on South Africa's railway and harbors. The government of Lesotho was blockaded recently and consequently overthrown. We in Zimbabwe are paying heavily for our endeavors to reorient our traffic from South African ports to Mozambican ports.

At the military level, South Africa supports all the bandit and dissident groups in the region. Where the bandit groups are not making sufficient headway, the South African defense forces resort to direct military action and occupation. The intention of the apartheid regime is quite clearly to install puppet regimes in the region by direct or indirect military or economic means. There are no simple solutions to these economic and military problems. One is dealing with a web of complex and complicated issues. Before the signing of the Nkomati Accord some people tended to believe the South African and American propaganda that signing a nonaggression pact would end all acts of aggression. In Zimbabwe, some people say if ZANU and ZAPU unite, the problem of dissidents and bandits will be resolved. But that argument ignores the fact that the real origin of dissidents is in the apartheid state. The scholars of the region should look at the systemic dynamics and avoid simplistic solutions that are not solutions at all in the long run.

The US policy of "constructive engagement" is merely the other side of the policy of destabilization. Not only does the American administration support the South African state, but it is now supporting bandit and dissident groups, calling them "freedom fighters," and it is actively undermining the position of independent African states. Under the direction of the US administration, the implementation of Resolution 435 on the independence of Namibia, could now be used as a platform for strengthening the hand of South Africa in the region and weakening the progressive forces.

The Association of African Political Scientists (AAPS) should now be recognized by the United Nations and the OAU as an important nongovernmental organization that brings together scholars from all regions of Africa and engages in useful policy-oriented research activities. Faced with the problems of southern Africa, AAPS itself should assist in building the agenda for the action that is already taking place. Our enemies are on the move and in action. We are on the move and in action also, but are we taking the right steps to defend ourselves and to achieve freedom and nationhood for Namibia and South Africa? In setting out an action-oriented agenda, AAPS should involve South African academics both from inside and outside South Africa. Most academics within South Africa are equally opposed to the apartheid state. They should be politicized and mobilized against the system. They could also help us in the information campaign against the regime by supplying vital information on the work of the resistance movement there.

1

Introduction

Bernard Magubane and Ibbo Mandaza

The revolution is not a magical act by this or that 'leader.' . . . The revolution is the sum of varied and diverse circumstances, of multiplex elements that together add up and lead to the solution in a given historical moment of a crisis that has stubborn and deep economic causes.

> —G.M. Serrati, cited by Fammett,
> *Antonio Gramsci and the Origins
> of Italian Communism*, p. 135.

Events in South Africa progress inexorably toward a climax that none but the blind can fail to recognize: the end of white minority rule. In March 1986 the Association of African Political Scientists (AAPS) sponsored a conference: *Whither South Africa?* The essays that follow are some of the papers presented at this symposium. The also mostly present views of black South Africans who seldom meet to discuss the problems of their country. These scholars represent various political tendencies in South Africa. The main objective of the symposium was not to achieve a consensus, but to provide a forum in which an informed discussion could take place.

The timing of the conference was also crucial. It was almost ten years since the collapse of Portuguese colonialism which caused a major breach in the white stronghold. June 16 would soon be at hand and blacks in South Africa were preparing to observe the 10th anniversary of the Soweto Uprising with major demonstrations. The Zimbabwe that Ian Smith had vowed in 1965 would never see black majority rule in his lifetime, or, indeed, in a thousand years, had achieved its independence under black rule in 1980. So, it was time to take stock and assess the achievements and hurdles that still lay ahead.

The conference was viewed as part of the ongoing effort to review the progress and difficulties faced by the liberation movement in South Africa and Namibia. The papers and panels covered many important topics that relate to various aspects of southern Africa. The conference proved to be a milestone and a significant step in clarifying many empirical and theoretical issues on the nature of white minority rule, its relation to imperialism, and the prospect for the liberation movement.

THE ORIGIN OF WHITE MINORITY RULE

To understand the current conjuncture requires first of all a clear understanding both of its origin and its nature. Accordingly the first issue to be addressed was the roots of the South African political economy and of the background to the formation of the Union as a white minority state. The origins of white minority rule, as will be obvious from reading the various contributions, attracted the attention of almost all the participants at the conference. White minority rule itself was seen as a beneficiary and guardian of imperialism and a peculiar kind of state that emerged after conquest and which excludes almost seventy-five percent of the indigenous peoples. The twin foundations of white minority rule are national oppression underwritten by racism, and class oppression rooted in the very origins of settler colonialism. With the conquest and plunder of the indigenous peoples, the enslavement and peonage of the slaves from Malaya, Mauritius, and elsewhere, and the indenture of "coolies" from India, racial and national oppression have been at the heart of class formation and the struggle for social emancipation in South Africa.

TO WHOM DOES SOUTH AFRICA BELONG?

In spite of the wars of conquest and dispossession and the attempts by the apartheid state to rob people of their citizenship rights in the land of their birth, Magubane argues, South Africa belongs to blacks, not because they are the numerical majority but because they constitute its labor force. The roots of apartheid's political economy, Magubane shows, goes back in history to the establishment of the Cape Colony, which pursued a dual policy of conquest and dispossession. The Khoisan and other indigenous peoples, having been deprived of their means of subsistence, were either completely destroyed or reduced to an indigent class forced to work for the Dutch East India Company and the wine farmers. With the advent of British colonialism the juggernaut of settler colonialism continued its conquest and devastation and became even more inextricably intertwined with the extension of capitalist property relations.

Capitalism, which in its classical expression rested on free labor and had no meaning apart from it, in South Africa conquered, enslaved, and indeed reinforced servile labor on an unprecedented scale. The general consensus in the conference was that to understand the nature of the settler society in its relations with the indigenous peoples, including all those who are considered "non-white," there was need to identify the motive force to its political economy—that is, how it developed and what form the process of capital accumulation took. Magubane's paper periodizes and lays bare the fundamental laws of motion of the process of capital accumulation in South Africa. He shows how, subject to the most severe restrictions, the incorporation and exploitation of black labor laid the basis for accumulation in each phase that the settler economy passed through.

As Africans lost their lands, they were spared the fate of American Indians and indigenous peoples in other settler colonies because their labor power was considered critical. In the meantime political machinery was put in place based on experience in divorcing labor from its means of subsistence that had been used in the metropolitan countries. Marx's study of the colonial problems had given him additional background material for examining important aspects of the capitalist mode of production. He came to the conclusion that colonial policy was a reflection of the most disgusting and bloodthirsty aspects of the capitalist system. About British rule in India, Marx wrote:

> The profound hypocrisy and inherent barbarism of bourgeois civilization lies unveiled before our eyes, turning from its home, where it assumes respectable forms, to the colonies, where it goes naked.[1]

This seems an apt description of what happened in South Africa as African people were conquered and incorporated within the orbit of the British empire. White settlers in South Africa "employed all the existing machinery of despotism to squeeze from [African] people the utmost might of contribution, the last dregs of their labor."[2] As in India, so largely in South Africa, all senior posts in the colonial administration, the judiciary, and the army—a vast parasitic tumor—were filled by the British, and this emphasized the deprived state of the conquered Africans.

What happened to the Africans in South Africa is not some new and unique thing. Karl Marx, elsewhere in his writing, explains that

> A conquering people divides the land among the conquerors, establishing thereby a certain division and form of landed property and determining the character of production, or it turns the conquered people into slaves and thus makes slave labour the basis of production. . . . Or legislation perpetuates land ownership in large families or distributes labour as a hereditary privilege and thus fixes it in castes.[3]

And just before the turn of the nineteenth century, J.A. Hobson, looking back at the history of the colonization movement, commented:

> Whenever superior races settle on lands where lower races can be profitably used for manual labour in agriculture, mining and domestic work, the latter do not tend to die out, but to form a servile class. This is the case, not only in tropical countries where white men cannot form real colonies, working and rearing families with safety and efficiency, and where hard manual work, if done at all, must be done by "coloured men", but even in countries where white men can settle, as in part of South Africa and of the southern portion of the United States.[4]

In every phase of settler capitalist development, from its emergence to its monopoly phase, race and class have been inextricably and inseparably intertwined. Primitive accumulation involved internal national conquest and dispossession of the African peoples. The creation and consolidation of cheap labor necessitated the repudiation of bourgeois democratic principle, that is, the denial of franchise rights to the majority of the people.

And today not only does the race factor continue to play a dominant role at the level of the relations of production, but also the very survival of the ruling class—its continued monopolistic hold on the land, mines and other means of production—

depends upon maintaining and even reinforcing the mechanisms which guarantee White race political control and domination.[5]

The question of who South Africa belongs to can be answered by raising two other questions: How did it become a "white man's" country? and What will genuine freedom imply in South Africa? There is an inseparable link in South Africa between the past and present and between national liberation and social emancipation. The dialectical process of conquest and dispossession necessarily implies a strategy which must lead to the revolutionary overthrow of the existing ruling class, and the complete dismantling and replacement of the white minority state apparatus.[6]

The historical study of institutionalized racial oppression reveals that it is inherent in the social, economic, political, and military structures of minority rule. Although today apartheid is regarded throughout the world, first and foremost, as a system of scandalously arbitrary rule, one of its major objectives is to secure white dominance, that is, retain South Africa as a "white man's" country and provide South African capitalists and their imperialist allies with resources and cheap labor.

White minority rule is an oppressive system which, systematically and simultaneously, exploits and oppresses blacks regardless of their status. Magubane examines the methods whereby the Dutch and British colonists imposed a racial hierarchy on the indigenous peoples. They also examine the implication of the role of British finance capital in fostering a cheap labor policy. This cheap labor policy intertwined and meshed with a racist ideology whose history is well known. The policies of Sir Alfred Milner, Cecil John Rhodes, and Social Darwinists reveal the scope of human intentionality—e.g., a systematic patterning of economic disadvantages which set black workers apart from their white counter parts.

RACE, CLASS, AND ETHNICITY

No question is therefore more central to the liberation movement in South Africa than that of racism and racial oppression. The reality of the qualitatively different conditions of life between blacks and whites that flow from the division of society based on "race" are well known. As a result, an understanding of the relationship between race and class in South Africa and the political implications of the struggle against class and racial oppression has long exercised the minds of scholars and politicians. Most of the contributors focus on the triple question of race, class, and ethnicity. As they point out, the study of race, class, and ethnicity has in many ways been the most theoretically confusing. The essentialist view of race and class adopted by liberal writers and by left writers is criticized by Magubane.

Any study of race, class, and ethnicity faces a key dilemma of the social sciences: how to reconcile a diachronic and a synchronic perspective. As Perry Anderson has pointed out, the reconciliation of history and sociology is easy enough in principle, but extremely hard in practice. "It will be remembered," he writes,

> that deSaussure defined a diachronic order as one in which each 'moment' can be only understood in terms of all those which have preceded it: thus, in a bridge game, the meaning of a trick depends on all the tricks before it and cannot be understood without knowledge of them. In contrast, a synchronic order is one in which the meaning of every moment is visible in the present: it is co-existensive with the relationship of all existing data to each other. . . . It is clear that any society has both these dimensions; it is at once a structure which can only be understood in terms of the inter-relationship of its parts, and a *process* which can only be understood in terms of the cumulative weight of its past. The difficult thing is to synthesize the two aspects in an actual study.[7]

Just as there is no abstract class society unrelated to its specific historical origins, so there is no capitalist society whose classes conform to the model Marx described in *Capital*. In our view an analysis of class, race, and ethnic relations in South Africa needs to grasp the historical particularity of that society. What is the significance, for instance, in South Africa of the division of the so-called "non-whites" into "Coloureds," Indians, and Africans, and the further subdivision of the Africans into ethnic and/or "tribal" entities? That is, the theoretical challenge becomes one of grasping other social questions, especially the age-old desire of the white minority to keep the oppressed fragmented and/or to divide—and—rule.

There is plenty of historical evidence indicating that the white settlers have always been haunted by the spectre of unity among those they exploit. In South Africa the particularity of the political division of the society along racial, class, and ethnic lines is to keep the oppressed hostile to each other. The obverse side of black fragmentation is the building of a white united front. Therefore the ideology of white supremacy serves first to create a white power bloc and second to identify the interests of their power bloc, including the white working class, with the interests of the capitalist class. The white workers are protected from experiencing the worst burdens of capitalist exploitation. Martin Legassick writes that

> The economic rule of the apartheid system (and its permutations) is to sustain cheap black labour. Simultaneously the apartheid system operates politically and ideologically to sustain "white unity" and divisions among the black oppressed. The stress placed by the ruling class on the preservation of "white identity" and "white minority interests" represents their need to maintain the coherence of the state machine—as the means of enforcing the cheap labour system.[8]

Racial dominance forms a basis for interclass solidarity within the dominant groups. The racial privilege enjoyed by the white workers at the expense of the black workers ties them politically and ideologically to the bourgeoisie on the basis of kith and kin, and provides one of the most stubborn features in the South African working class.

To explain the white united front, Magubane has resurrected Lenin's theory of the labor aristocracy, showing through the history and particularities of South Africa how the labor aristocracy became part of the white united front. Briefly, Lenin, it will will be remembered, asked and answered the question that is often confused by those adopting an essentialist view of class: the nature of relations between workers of the dominant and subordinate groups in a situation like South Africa. Lenin asked and answered the key question on the race/class dialectic in social formations, which are structured on the basis of white supremacy, as follows:

> Is the actual condition of the workers in the oppressor and in the oppressed nations the same, from the standpoint of the national question?
>
> No, it is not the same.
>
> 1. *Economically*, the difference is that sections of the working class in the oppressor nations receive the crumbs from the *super profits* the bourgeoisie of these nations obtained by extra exploitation of the workers of the oppressd nations. Besides, the economic statistics show that there a *larger* percentage of the workers become "straw bosses" than is the case in the oppressed nations. A *larger* percentage rise to the labour *aristocracy*. This is a fact. *To a certain degree* the workers of the oppressor nations are

partners of their own bourgeoisie in plundering the workers (and the mass of the population) of the oppressed nations.

2. *Politically*, the difference is that, compared with the workers of the oppressed nations, they occupy a privileged position in many spheres of political life.

3. *Ideologically*, or spiritually, the difference is that they are taught, at school and in life, disdain and contempt of all the workers of the oppressed nations. . . . Thus *all along the line* there are differences in the objective world that is independent of the will and consciousness of individuals [emphases added].[9]

There is the subtle rub: white workers are bribed effectively by their ruling class. Lenin was not the first to understand the corrupting influence of the doctrine of white supremacy. With great sorrow and regret, DuBois wrote about white workers in the United States: "Were they not lordly Whites and should they not share in the spoils of rape? High wages in the United States and England might be skillfully manipulated results of slavery in Africa and of peonage in Asia."[10]

THE NATURE OF THE SOUTH AFRICAN STATE

The previous discussion has partly preempted our consideration of the state; nevertheless we must look at the nature of the white settler state more closely. The current upsurge in the struggle for freedom in South Africa and the murderous response of the army and the police has raised anew the question of the nature and character of the white minority state. The destruction of the organs of support which the white minority state relied upon within the black community has all but paralyzed the authority of the regime. The flight of the black policemen from their homes in townships, the rejection and defeat of the community council system, the inability of the state to collect rent, the emergence of the street committees—all point to the paralysis of a part of the administrative machinery of the state. This development challenges whatever legitimacy the regime had.

The only way in which white minority rule can be "maintained" is through the use of emergency powers of the state. On June 12, 1986, the Botha regime declared a state of emergency covering the whole country. The decree is described by *Newsweek* (June 23, 1986) as

. . . a classic example of Afrikaner logic—effectively giving ruthlessness the force of law. The order is a turgid, technically worded cover for giving the government power to arrest anyone it wants. Police can detain, without warrant, any person who they believe might pose a threat to public order. They can keep suspects in jail for up to two weeks without charges or trial. The regulations make it illegal to disclose the names of detained people, to record or disseminate "subversive" statements or to report on public violence. They even outlaw any bid to "aggravate feelings of hostility in the public"—including any attempt to speculate about when the state of emergency might end. Violators of the order face up to a $7,200 fine or 10 years in prison.

The state of emergency will become a permanent feature of South Africa in terms of the "amendment" of the Public Safety Act recently adopted by parliament and the Internal Security Act. That is, the "regime" is trying to resolve the problems of illegitimacy with machine guns and revolvers.

African townships today are occupied by troops as if they were foreign territories. This development reveals the true nature of relations between Africans and their erstwhile rulers. George Bernard Shaw described South Africa more than half a century ago as a "slave state."[11] The limited rights and freedoms of the black people which prompted him to make that remark have been reduced even further, while their labor power has become even more indispensable for the economy of the country. When Basil Davidson describes South Africa as not a slave state, but "a state of organized servitude,"[12] he is not exaggerating.

The fundamental political question facing blacks concerns their relation to the apartheid state. Lenin, following Marx and Engels, had defined the state as a "special organization of force; the organization of violence for the suppression of some class." In South Africa the state intervenes in all aspects of black struggles in its efforts to check the growth of independent political will and power; it controls individual Africans through the Pass Laws which insure that every employer has his complement of servile black labor; it uses its laws against "communism," "sabotage," and "terrorism" in order to repress black political activity. Now with the new laws that have been just passed, the suppression of every form of political organization and opposition to apartheid is to be pursued with still greater zeal and intensity.

The roots of the apartheid state go back in history and have their origin in the fact that European settlers, as a result of technological developments, acquired the means not only to conquer African chiefdoms and kingdoms but to ensure the conditions of their subjection. The emergence of the colonial state cannot be separated from the extension of capitalist property relations, which with the arrival of the British settlers in the early part of the 19th century became dominant. With the discovery of diamond and gold mines, the settler-colonial state, as Mafeje points out, had to be consolidated. The economic role of the states which united the four settler colonies of the Cape, Natal, The Orange Free State and the Transvaal in 1910 (and its permutations) was to sustain cheap black labor. Simultaneously the Union, based as it was on the Boer and British colonist, would operate politically and ideologically to consolidate a white united front while creating divisions among the black oppressed. The state plays a role in the consolidation and political unification of capital in the face of its economic divisions through the constitution of a unified power bloc. At the same time it works to disunify and demobilize the popular masses, as well as encourage their active support through granting limited concessions and fostering ideological illusions.[13] The importance Milner attached to elevating all whites, including workers, to a level above all Africans represented a conscious effort by Britism imperialism to maintain the coherence of the white settlers as a ruling oligarchy— while also securing capital in the masses of cheap black labor.

In South Africa the role of the state in constituting classes is very evident. This means that the notions about the neutrality of the productive forces must be qualified. The South African capitalist economy is not a field ruled by the logic of its own economic laws with politics something located outside it. Instead, the economy, like other levels, is a terrain of political struggle governed not by a simple economic logic alone, but by the hegemonic articulation of social forces in society as a whole, mediated through the economic structure.[14]

Echoing Milner, the 1913 Select Committee Report argued that

> . . . the European minority, occupying, as it does in relation to the non-European majority, the position of a dominant aristocracy . . . cannot allow a considerable number of its members to sink into apathetic indigency. . . . If they do and they manifest an indifference founded on the comfortable doctrine of letting things find their economic level, sooner or later, notwithstanding all our material and intellectual advantages, our race is bound to perish in South Africa.[15]

It is important to realize that, so far as the ruling class was concerned, "white domination" was seen as the guarantor of stability.

Capitalist private property does not consist in things—things exist independently of ownership—but in a social relation between people. Property confers upon its owners freedom from labor and the disposal of the labor of others, and this is the essence of all social domination, whatever form it may take. It follows that the protection of property is fundamentally the assurance of social domination to owners over non-owners. And this, in turn, is precisely what is meant by class domination, which is the primary function of the state.[16]

THE THEORY OF INTERNAL COLONIALISM AND THE SOUTH AFRICAN STATE

The key theoretical and legal question Jordan's thesis raises is whether South Africa is an independent and sovereign state. This question does not dispose of the political and social question. That is, is the existing South African state a legitimate representative of the people? Further, this question does not dispose of the question whether the South African state should be recognized diplomatically and associated with as a normal part of the community of nations.[17]

Like the "Native Republic" of the 1920s, the internal colonialism thesis spells out the duality of South Africa. The most important theoretical contribution of the internal colonialism thesis is that it lays bare the symbiotic relationship between material oppression and capitalist exploitation. In the "Native Republic" thesis, Pallo Jordan points out that the national and class dimensions were seen as inseparable, that neither can be stressed at the expense of the other; they must be read together. "This was a theoretical departure which was to have the most profound implications once it was grasped by the liberation movement."[18]

Jack Barnes agrees with the internal colonialism thesis when he writes that

> The state in South Africa—this capitalist state is not a national state, at least not in the meaningful sense of the term. Only a small minority in South Africa has any right of citizenship. This minority—some 5 million out of a total population of about 33 million—is defined by law as persons of the white race. There is no South African *nation-state*; there is a state of the "white race." In the geographical territory that the apartheid state controls, in

what is today the *country* of South Africa, the overwhelming majority of people have no constitutional rights to speak of. Blacks are effectively denied the right to citizenship in the country in which they live and work.[19]

It was in response to this exclusive "white" state that the Native National Congress was formed in 1912 (later to transform itself into the African National Congress of South Africa [ANC]). Today under the leadership of the South African National Liberation Movement, the working class and other oppressed classes are launching their most powerful assault yet against the exclusionary state in South Africa. Out of the defeat suffered by African peasants and workers in the early part of this century arose the phoenix of the future.[20]

Following the Sharpeville massacre, the ANC and the PAC were banned. In summarizing the lessons of the 1980s, especially the massacre and the banning, it was concluded that only armed struggle would lead to liberation. One of the peculiarities of South Africa, as we have said, is that written into its structure is not only the systematic national oppression of all blacks, but the endemic violence that is used against the black population. Fanon had already recognized that settler-state violence was a structural imperative by which such an unnatural order could be maintained and indeed perpetuated. As he put it, in such societies the state is not a "thinking machine": it epitomizes violence in its "natural state" and it can only be confronted and terminated by revolutionary counterviolence.[21] The ANC as a "national" liberation movement is, by definition, a political process, involving whatever political means are dictated by the prevailing situation, to wrest the political, economic, and social power of the country from the hands of a "foreign" minority and place them under the rule of the majority.

Because national oppression and capitalist exploitation are inextricably intertwined in South Africa, national liberation is thus part of a socialist program even though it is not, itself, socialist. Basically, the South African National Liberation Movement is part of the democratic program which, if it is to be successful, must be advanced by the working class and within which the working class must assume a large role. As Lenin put it:

> The proletariat cannot be victorious except through democracy, i.e., by introducing complete democracy and by combining every step of its struggle with democratic demands formulated in the most determined manner. It is absurd to contrast the socialist

revolution and the revolutionary struggle against capitalism with *one* of the questions of democracy, in this case, the national question. We must *combine* the revolutionary struggle against capitalism with a revolutionary programme and revolutionary tactics relative to *all* democratic demands: a republic, a militia, election of officials by the people, equal rights for women, self-determination of nations, etc. While capitalism exists, these demands can be achieved only in exceptional cases, and in an incomplete, distorted form. Basing ourselves on democracy as already achieved, exposing its incompleteness under capitalism, we demand the overthrow of capitalism, the expropriation of the bourgeoisie, as a necessary basis both for the abolition of the poverty of the masses and for the *complete* and *all-sided* achievement of *all* democratic reforms. Some of these reforms will be started before the overthrow of the bourgeoisie, others *in the process* of this overthrow, and still others after it. The social revolution is not a single battle, but represents a whole epoch of numerous battles around all the problems of economic and democratic reforms, which can be consummated only by the expropriation of the bourgeoisie. It is for the sake of this final aim that we must formulate *every one* of our democratic demands in a consistently revolutionary manner. It is quite conceivable that the workers of a certain country may overthrow the bourgeoisie *before* even one fundamental democratic reform has been accomplished in full. It is entirely inconceivable, however, that the proletariat, as a historical class, will be able to defeat the bourgeoisie if it is not prepared for this task by being educated in the spirit of the most consistent and determinedly revolutionary democracy.[22]

In the context of the national liberation movement, the working class must become part of the united front that fights for independence and, if possible, it must be the vanguard of this movement. To the extent that it is so organized and does command a leadership position, to that extent will the struggle for national liberation advance uninterrupted to achieve social liberation.

When the settler community is strong, the racist state has its political advantage. When challenged by the oppressed it could unleash bloody violence without being hampered by any articulate parliamentary opposition. In its agony, however, the racist state faces a dilemma. That is why the regime is now seeking to detach "Coloureds" and Indians from the growing Black United Front, and also trying to find a formula to integrate a few "representative" blacks into its parliament. The regime has even made it a crime to refer to the state as a "white minority state"!

The Women Question

The oppression of women and the place which women occupy in the struggle for national emancipation and for social and economic equality has come to the forefront of contemporary social struggles. The women's struggle develops beside and interacts with other social questions—against classism and racism. The participation of women in these struggles has often provided that critical margin between victory and defeat.

Ivy Matsepe's contribution raises some critical questions about the situation of the black woman in South Africa. She argues that male power is materialized in various practices and in the vocabularies through which power is articulated and which play a role in its constitution and reproduction. The oppression of women is reproduced not only in the economy, politics, and ideology, but also through apparatuses like the family, practices like marriage, and manifold ideologies like sexism—in short, the entire system of patriarchy.

Matsepe focuses on the forces in South Africa through which women in general, and black women in particular, are forced into positions of dependence and inequality. She shows that at the base of this process lie changes in the capitalist mode of production introduced by white settlers. In South Africa, for instance, the wife of a black miner whose husband works as a migrant laborer, and is forced to eke out a miserable existence scratching the parched earth, subsidizes through her unrequited labor the mining profits of mining monopolies. Take another example: if she is employed as a domestic servant in a white household in any city, she is not only subject to exploitation by her white employer, but, because of influx control laws, she cannot have a normal family. Her living conditions do not make provision for her husband and children. In addition, as a domestic servant, she frees her employer to take better-paying jobs in industry. Furthermore she is likely to be exposed to sexual exploitation by the husband of her employer. Her exploitation and oppression are multidimensional.

That is, "the inequality and oppression of black women runs the gamut from the most gross and brutalizing experiences to the more insidious."[23] The most important theoretical challenge is finding the connecting concept that sums up the diverse modes of oppression and exploitation. In South Africa it is often said that black women suffer triple oppression: as blacks, as women, and as workers.[24] As Gaitskell, et al point out,

> Domestic service compromises one of the major sources of wage employment for African women in South Africa, and it is an important nexus of this triple oppression. The meaning of triple oppression is complex. It does not simply represent a convergence or "coalescence" of three distinct types of oppression, seen as variables which can be analysed in isolation from each other and then superimposed. Sexual subordination when one is racially subordinate is one thing. Sexual subordination when one is a wage laborer in a racist society is quite another. In South Africa can there be a unity based on gender? What are the political "boundaries of sisterhood?" Like everything else in South Africa an understanding of the historical and material conditions of Blacks and women under conditions of internal colonialism shows that "triple oppression" is a very complex condition.[25]

Consequently, although all women experience inequality relative to the men of their class, there is a vast differential in the overall conditions of life and actual substance of the oppression women experience depending upon their class membership and whether their husbands have permanent urban residence or whether they are migrants. Clarity on all these issues, Matsepe argues, is extremely important for the consideration of the liberation movement.

THE INTERNATIONAL CONTEXT

The white minority regime in South Africa is not only economically but politically dependent on the existence of the British empire. The political oppression and economic exploitation of the black population benefitted the bourgeoisie of a few Western imperialist countries and their local counterparts. South Africa is organically integrated into the capitalist world system. This means that the economic and social structure of the country is governed by the laws of this system and is controlled by the classes that dominate the world market. As Blackburn puts it: "Throughout Southern Africa colonialist and racist regimes thrived within the capitalist world community and were supported by the military alliance."[26]

The contributions by Nolutshungu and Mandaza deal with the economic, political, and military aspects of South Africa's integration into the world economy, and imperialist strategies to protect what they like to call their "strategic" interest in southern Africa. Because of the character of the impending revolution in South Africa and the immense stakes in its outcome for the imperialist powers, the current upsurge in South Africa is having a deep impact in the Western capitals. Those who formulate Western response to the unfolding revolutionary situation in South Africa consciously or unconsciously understand that the struggle there is an integral part of the worldwide revolutionary struggle.

The imperialist monopolies in South Africa represent huge concentrations of capital. By the turn of the twentieth century the integration of the country economically had reached an extremely advanced stage. Its diamond and gold mining industries were organized directly in terms of ties to the world economy and South Africa's relations with British and Portuguese colonies. This is the context in which both Nolutshungu and Mandaza view the dilemma the South African State faces and the contradictions of the imperialist powers. For imperialism, South Africa is a crucial power in many respects. It is by far the most economically developed country in Africa, and it occupies a strategic position as a supplier of indispensable scarce metals to the world market. Its system of racial segregation and repression is a veritable paradigm of capitalist superexploitation. It has a white monopoly capitalist ruling class and an advanced black proletariat. It is so far the only country with a well-developed, modern capitalist structure which is not only "objectively" ripe for revolution but has actually entered a stage of overt and seemingly irreversible revolutionary struggle.[27]

These and other attributes and characteristics of South Africa serve to emphasize that there is no other country in the world that has anything like the material and symbolic significance of South Africa for the liberation forces and those who have vested interests in the status quo. "A victory for the revolution, i.e., a genuine and lasting change in basic power relations in South Africa would have an impact on the balance of global forces comparable to that of the wave that followed World War II."[28]

The imperialist powers may "abhor" apartheid, and indeed have expressed fear that it will collapse in disaster; but come what may, they find they have no "choice" but to stand by their initial interest, that is, they must defend the white minority regime and defy world public opinion. For "the West" to abandon the Botha regime now, its leaders believe, would be to encourage the creation of a new South Africa independent of their influence. South Africa today is the Frankenstein Monster that roams the corridors of the White House and 10 Downing

Street.[29] How to tame this monster is a quandry for Reagan and Thatcher![30]

As the final phase of revolutionary tremors shake the white minority to its foundations, the importance of the settler state controlling the black majority is becoming clear, internally and internationally. The morale of the ruling classes is being sapped. On the international front, diplomatic coordination and maneuvering isolates the white minority regime more and more before world public opinion. Internally, the divestment campaign dries up economic investment. Confronted by this dual process of internationalization, the nerves of the settler regime are stretched to the breaking point. Talk of negotiations abound, causing upheaval in the ranks of the regime. What the London *Economist* calls degenerative collapse seems to be the direction South Africa is heading.

WHITHER SOUTH AFRICA?

The question "Whither South Africa?" is a difficult one for the analyst, whose task by nature is neither to predict nor to prophesy the course and outcome of such complex historical processes. All the analysts in this book express their faith in the ultimate and inevitable victory of the liberation forces in South Africa. But they do so on the basis of analyses that expose the fundamental contradictions within the history and development of South Africa.

The first of these basic contradictions is the imposition and development of white settler colonialism in an African country on the one hand; and on the other the incessant resistance of the African peoples, from the very inception of foreign domination in 1652 to the present day. The 300 years of struggle are in themselves evidence of a course of historical and economic development that has brought to the fore different classes and forces in the South African social formation. The complexity of this colonial situation is quite obvious. But three particular themes stand out and broadly indicate the possible outcome of the current conjuncture in South Africa: (1) the nature of the South African settler colonial state, i.e., its class composition and its linkage with the imperialist forces of international finance capital; and (2) the overall strategic and economic interests of the US imperialists and their allies in southern Africa in general and South Africa in particular. The symbiotic relationship between imperialism and white settler colonialism accounts for this particular expression of domination, rendering the apartheid state for a long time almost invincible, lasting, and seemingly even permanent. But even as the forces of African resistance have been sustained and developed into an avalanche that now threatens to sweep away apartheid, the white settler colonial state still appears intransigent and full of fight. The role of the imperialist forces in this struggle is not only a factor but a crucial determinant in the current conjuncture in which imperialist hegemony appears so dominant.

A second contradiction is the relationship between race, class, and ethnicity; and how this, in turn, impinges on the discussion of the struggle for national liberation. It is enough that racism is already a crucial feature in the characterization of the apartheid state and its ability to hold together all the white classes in defense of white minority rule. But African nationalism has its roots in this century-old ideology of white supremacy and in colonialist oppression and exploitation. It is both an inspiration for social and political action in the struggle for African liberation and an impediment, on the part of its adherents, to the understanding of imperialism and its neocolonial strategies. But it also raises important questions about the nature, direction, and outcome of the struggle against apartheid. Even the theoretical debate on this has to begin with an acknowledgement of the reality of African nationalism in the South African struggle. As has been pointed out elsewhere,[31] African nationalism is the indispensable force in the movement for national liberation; and yet it is also the basis for the neocolonialism by which the masses are betrayed. The apparent irony in this historical process should not however lead us into the kind of analyses that dismiss nationalist movements as merely movements of the African petit-bourgeoisie and not those of the masses. The point, however, is that African nationalism—and the African petit-bourgeoisie—remains at the center of Africa's quest for total liberation, for the reassertion of African dignity, for Africa's return to history.

The fact of apartheid South Africa remains a symbol of Africa's unique historical experience as a continent—and those in diaspora—which has had to endure overall oppression and exploitation almost on the basis of color. By its very strength and dominance, African nationalist ideology will tend to disguise the class structure of African societies, tend to hide the reality of the class struggle, and even thereby tend to reinforce neocolonialism. But these are all issues to be examined and confronted in analyses of African societies; we cannot resolve them by running away from them.[32]

This leads us to a third historical contradiction raised by the question "Whither South Africa?" The backlog of the Zimbabwe situation is pertinent in that it reveals the extent to which imperialist strategies can and will seek to forestall the logic of the protracted struggle in southern Africa. The current US policy in the subregion has to be understood in the context of such objectives. These are some of the issues raised in Mandaza's paper. But before referring to the latest US pronouncements in this regard, it is important also to consider the nature of the liberation movement itself, its history, its class composition, and its ideological content. It has been possible to deal with this question only briefly in this book. No doubt future analyses will examine these and related issues more incisively. For the analysis of the post–white settler colonial state in Zimbabwe[33] underlines the need to examine the pre-independence phase of the struggle more closely; taking into account not only the military, political, and ideological capacity of the national liberation movement but also the danger of intra-nationalist and ethnic rivalry which enemies of the struggle can exploit for their own ends so as to render the national liberation movement vulnerable to last-minute compromises.

Mandaza's paper warned in March 1986 of the danger that South Africa and its US ally will try not only to balkanize but also to cause disunity and thus impede the national liberation movement. His paper sought to illustrate the growing US involvement in southern Africa, raising the possibility of a negotiated settlement in South Africa. Both the recent developments in the subregion and the pronouncements of the US Government in July 1986 would seem to confirm the concern which Mandaza's paper raised in March. The situation in southern Africa is so dynamic and yet also predictable in terms of what to expect of an enemy on the defense. Thus, Reagan's recent pronouncement[34] on the South African situation is yet another reaffirmation of the US strategy in the subregion, an imperial claim on African and its resources, and a statement of the belief that southern Africa in general—and South Africa in particular—is a US sphere of influence:

In Southern Africa, our national ideals and strategic interests come together. . . . Strategically, this is one of the most vital regions of the world. Around the Cape of Good Hope passes the oil of the Persian Gulf—which is indispensable to the industrial economies of Western Europe. Southern Africa and South Africa are [the] repository of many of the vital minerals—vanadium, manganese, chromium, platinum—for which the West has no other secure source of supply. If this rising hostility in Southern Africa—between Pretoria and the front-line States—explodes, the Soviet Union will be the main beneficiary. And the critical ocean corridor of South Africa, and the strategic minerals of the region, would be at risk.[35]

Unemployment among urban blacks now stands at 25 percent, and runs over 50 percent in some urban areas. And, for the first time since the National Party came to power, white unemployment is a serious problem. From March 1985 to March of this year, 40,000 whites lost their jobs. There are over 250,000 new job seekers in South Africa every year; the economy needs a real growth rate of 5 percent just to keep unemployment at current levels. With no growth in prospect, the country cannot create jobs for either blacks or whites.

Later, on August 13th, Reagan agreed with Botha on the idea of an international conference to guarantee peace and security in the southern African subregion.[41]

There are many factors—including a rear base (the Frontline States) that is also in favor of a negotiated settlement—that might influence the National Liberation Movement to accept a compromise. But let's suppose the situation becomes even more complex than it is and that the liberation forces continue as relentlessly as we would expect; what is the likely reaction of the US imperialists and their allies? And what is likely to be the reaction of the Frontline States when they inevitably find the war situation unbearable and threatening to the security of their states? And how will the various classes and forces within the South African situation—including the liberation movement—react in the light of a protracted war and given the nature of imperialist and bourgeois hegemony in South Africa?

These are questions that have to be answered in the process of the liberation struggle itself, and no doubt the National Liberation Movement will be acutely aware of these issues as they plan and implement the war. Much will hinge on the relationship between the internal and external forces within the liberation movement itself and how the latter can define and develop its motive force and anchor around the working class and other mass movements within South Africa. The task of the committed analyst is therefore to try to unravel the complex nature of the historical, political, and socio-economic process in such a way as to inspire, support, and enjoin those of our comrades that are locked in real battles with the enemies of the African people. These essays are an attempt to do just that.

NOTES

1. *Karl Marx, A Biography,* Prepared by the Marxist–Leninist Institute of the CPSU Central Committee, Progress Publishers, 1973, pp. 284–285.

2. *Ibid.*

3. Karl Marx, *The Grundrisse,* New York: Harper and Row, 1971, p. 29.

4. J.A. Hobson, *Imperialism,* Ann Arbor: The University of Michigan Press, 1965, p. 258.

5. Joe Slovo, "Reforms and Revolution in South Africa," *Sebacha,* February, 1985, p. 6.

6. *Ibid.,* p. 9.

7. Perry Anderson, "Portugal and the End of Ultra-Colonialism," *New Left Review,* 17(1962):113.

8. Martin Legassick, "South Africa: What Route to Democracy?," *African Affairs: A Journal of the Royal African Society,* 84.337(1985):594.

9. V.I. Lenin, *Collected Works,* Volume 23, pp. 55–56.

10. W.E.B. DuBois, *Dark Waters: Voices from Within the Vail,* New York: Schocken, 1920, p. 47.

11. George Bernard Shaw quoted by Basil Davidson, *South Africa:Progress or Disaster?,* Canon Collins Memorial Lecture, London: British Defence and Aid for Southern Africa, 1984, p. 13.

12. *Ibid.*

13. Paul Castello, "Antonio Gramsci and the Recasting of Marxist Strategy," *The Theoretical Review,* 31(1983):18.

14. *Ibid.,* p. 17.

15. Quoted by Robert Davis, *Capital, State and White Labour in South Africa 1900–1960: A Historical Materialist Analysis of Class Formation and Class Relations,* Atlantic Highlands: Humanities Press, 1979, p. 16.

16. Paul Sweezy, *The Theory of Capitalist Development,* New York: Monthly Review Press, 1942, pp. 243–246.

17. Joe Slovo, *op cit,* p. 7.

18. Pallo Jordan, *Socialist Transformation and the Freedom Charter,* Lusaka, Zambia: African National Congress Research Unit for the Southern Africa Universities, 1983, p. 10.

19. Jack Barnes, "The Coming Revolution in South Africa," *New International: A Magazine of Marxist Politics and Theory,* 2.2(1985):7–8.

20. Duncan Innes, *Anglo-Americans and the Life of Modern South Africa,* New York: Monthly Review Press, 1984.

21. Frantz Fanon, *The Wretched of the Earth,* Harmondsworth: Penguin Books, 1967.

22. Quoted in "National Liberation Movements and the Question of Socialism," *Science, Class and Politics,* 25:10–11.

23. Cf Linda Burnham and Miream Louis, "The Impossible Marriage: A Marxist Critique of Social Feminism," *Line of March: A Marxist-Leninist Journal of Rectification,* 7:6.

24. Gaitskell, Kimble, Maconachie, and Unterhalter, "Class, Race and Gender:

Domestic Workers in South Africa," *Review of African Political Economy*, 27/28(1984):86.

25. *Ibid.*, p. 87.
26. Robin Blackburn (ed.), *Revolution and Class Struggle: A Reader in Marxist Politics*, London: Fontana, 1977, p. 18.
27. Paul Sweezy and Harry Magdoff, "The Stakes in South Africa: Review of the Month," *Monthly Review*, 37.11(1986):4.
28. *Ibid.*, p. 6.
29. Cf Editorial, *The Nation*, 242.25(June 1984):876.
30. Mrs. Margaret Thatcher at a news conference in Canada (July 13, 1986), while hypocritically arguing that economic sanctions against South Africa would increase unemployment, starvation, and deprivation among blacks, finally admitted the reasons of her arguing against sanctions. She said that the West would expose itself to reliance on the Soviet Union for key strategic defense materials like platinum and chemical chrome. "Some of these materials are extremely important for our defence industries. People should think twice before they make statements about sanctions on South Africa which might jeopardise our capacity to have access to these fundamental raw materials" (*The Herald*, July 14, 1986).
31. Ibbo Mandaza, "Introduction," *Zimbabwe: The Political Economy of Transition 1980–1986*, Ed. by Ibbo Mandaza, Dakar, London, Harare: Codesria Book Series, 1986.
32. *Ibid.*
33. See Ibbo Mandaza, "The State in Post–White Settler Colonial Society," in Ibbo Mandaza (ed.), *op cit.*
34. Reagan's "Peace Plan for South Africa," USIS Special Report, July 22, 1986.
35. *Ibid.*
36. "US Aim is 'Better Future' for S. Africa," Statement to Senate Foreign Relations Committee, July 23, 1986.
37. *Time Magazine*, August 4, 1986.
38. US Secretary of State Robert Shultz, Statement to US Senate Foreign Relations Committee, July 23, 1986.
39. *Ibid.*
40. *Ibid.*
41. USIS, August 13, 1986.

2

South Africa:
The Dynamics of a Beleaguered State
Archie Mafeje

AN OVERVIEW: THEORETICAL AND HISTORICAL

Hardly any state in Africa has been a subject of so many theses as the South African state. Yet, we are not any wiser for it. Could it be, as some wit or nitwit (*niet weet*) has surmised, it is so full of nonsense that it beats the best minds? South African rulers often reply that "you have to be a South African to understand the reality of our country." Barely anybody would deny that authenticity is the ultimate test for truth. However, the only rub is that those who speak scarcely remember that authentic subjects are never formed but in contradiction, i.e., in any given situation there is more than one truth.

Thus, interacting subjects mutually create on another, whether in the positive or in the negative sense. In other words, it is the nature of ideological affirmations to be collective as well as exclusive or inward-looking. For instance, the South Africa of the Afrikaners is not the South Africa of so many other collectivities in the country. Even "our country" is not as self-evident as it sounds. In this context "reality" often turns out to be so many rationalizations or excuses for things which could be understood otherwise. Vested interest is what comes to mind immediately. This is not to say that symbols are less important

23

than what they stand for. On the contrary, they are the means for forging the necessary link between objects and subjects.

But symbols, like the subjects who manipulate them, operate at more than one level. The symbols used for deciphering universal history need not be the same as those used for deciphering local history. By now everyone is familiar with the distinction between "universal" language and "vernacular," especially in colonial countries. In the context of domination, universal languages are a supreme instrument for indoctrination and in the context of liberation, "vernacular" languages are a powerful instrument for self-assertion and self-rediscovery. Every politician or cadre knows this. In their moment of triumph—when Afrikaans became the official language in South Africa—the Afrikaners boasted as if to convince themselves: *"Die taaltjie is nou 'n taal"* (The little language is now a language). As is known, this is not the way universal languages are made. Think of Latin during the middle ages in Europe, French during the rise of the bourgeoisie, and English during the colonial and imperialist epoch. The truth is that Afrikaans is a vernacular which serves distinctly parochial interests. Therefore, the apparent or actual political hegemony of the Afrikaners over a wider social formation with universal dimensions is an anomaly and the basic cause of their social and political dilemma. "Upon this rock I shall build my Church." It is a question whether St. Peter was a founding hero or simply a trickster.

For the time being, seeing that we all exhibit the same ambiguity and pretension either as organic or synthetic intellectuals, it is important to clarify the status of our texts or syntexes. It is more or less acknowledged now that scientific languages, like ordinary languages, are capable of universalism as well as its opposite. It was only yesterday that structural-functionalism and behavioralism were parading as universal theories. It took a specifically Latin American paradigm, the *dependencia* "theory," to shatter that illusion. In the wake of these developments, one has heard repeated calls for the indigenization of the social sciences. While this is perfectly consistent and generally acceptable, it is clear that the left and the right in the affected regions are not agreed on the terms of reference. Nor is this simply a matter of theory. It is also a matter of political choices which are strongly contested among classes and within classes. The latter is particularly relevant to us with regard to the petit-bourgeoisie in Africa—a category which is crucial in our discourse and will receive fuller treatment later.

The relationship between theory and political choice or ideology is particularly intractable in the social sciences. This is so much so that the more reflective among social scientists have come to the inevitable conclusion that, methodologically, the social sciences are *incorrigible*, that is, they cannot be free of their subjective or ideological component (the implicit comparison with the other sciences need not concern us here). This raises questions regarding the distinction between universalism and "indigenism" (a vulgarism which does not appear even in the most low-brow English dictionary, thus leaving us with the ideologically-loaded term, "parochialism," that was so loved by the "modernization" theorists). This is directly related to the problem of authenticity in theoretical representations.

Since the beginning of the 1970s there has been a noticeable trend towards Marxist theory among African social scientists (and others), especially among political scientists in Africa. Whether this is reflective of the pliability of their relatively young discipline, the resurrection of political economy under the impact of the *dependencia* school, or of the primacy of political issues in the continent is something which is very difficult to determine. However, what is germane to our exploration is the fact that Marxism has universalistic pretensions and yet is founded on European history at a particular juncture. Slogans about "Marxism-Leninism," appealing as they are, cannot be offered as an epistemological explanation. If Marxism is a universal scientific theory, how does it overcome its own syntactical and semantic limitations? In other words, methodologically, how does it relate to vernacular languages understood in the analytical, political sense? Deep down, this might be the problem of every contemporary Marxist, though some pretend otherwise.

For South African organic intellectuals, the problem is even worse. It is *known*, but (out of political expediency) not often acknowledged, that the beginnings of Marxist theory and socialist politics in South Africa resulted from a transplant of the twenty-one points laid down by the Third International (or Comintern) for fraternal organizations everywhere in the world. But in fact Lenin and his party had designed these specifically for the leadership of the socialist movement in capitalist Europe, where schooled Marxists and an experienced working-class existed. In contrast, in South Africa there was a dearth of both the Marxist tradition and working-class politics. Neither the Jewish Bund nor the International League, the precursors of the Communist Party of South Africa (CPSA), could be looked upon as authentic local representatives. Not only did they look upon the African mine workers as "semi-savage" but they also reflected none of the great debates in Russia concerning the future of the peasant commune, as against what happened in Western Europe. The same shortcomings persisted after the foundation of the Communist Party of South Africa, as is evidenced by events during the 1922 miners' strike where some members of the CPSA joined white vigilantes to quell the "black menace."

Apologists see such recollections doing nobody any good. Naturally, if wishes were horses, we would all ride. These embarrassments are still very much with us. It would be idle to suppose that South African revolutionaries have lived down the problem of the relationship between universal and vernacular language. After the First World War, the African migrant workers in the mines spoke a different language, as they still do, from that prescribed by the Third or even the Fourth International. The European immigrant workers and intellectuals were more than presumptuous in assuming they were the natural or authentic interlocutors in the situation. As has been remarked, they were neither up-to-date with Marxist debates in Europe, nor adept in African political vernacular. Their imported notions of "tribal economy," "communal land tenure," "feudal landlords," and "peasants" were like semantic categories abstracted from another language. This resulted in two critical developments. First, the CPSA became very dependent, theoretically, on its Third International mentors, as is shown by the frequent visits of its leaders to Moscow for consultations and *instructions* which are still evident in its programs. Second, being unable to reach the "semi-tribal" black workers, it turned to the black petit-bourgeoisie who predominated in the African National Congress. The CPSA should have known from the beginning that this was the only class among the blacks in South Africa who comprehended both the vernacular and the universal language; they were the *natural* and *authentic* interlocutors.

These observations often provoke resentment or even hostility among South Africans. Yet, the lines of cleavage are not absolute. Our interest in raising the question at all is the ambiguity of the relationship between black and white in South Africa. One of the theses of the South African Communist party is that South Africa is an example of "internal colonialism by whites over blacks." This applies equally to the white immigrant mine workers at the beginning of the century and to the CPSA in the 1920s. Both groups wanted not only to impose on the black worker their imported language, but also reserve the right to "guide" them. Leo Marquard, a well-known South African liberal, espoused the same theory and advocated "white leadership with justice." Paradoxically enough, it is the Afrikaners, the acknowledged perpetrators of white colonialism in South Africa, who have no universal language to impose on the blacks and offer them no guidance to their green pastures. Instead, they fight in a *vernacular* language to exclude Africans from a white (bourgeois) civilization they themselves have never known since they disappeared into the Karroo in the middle of the 19th century. Thus, the class content of the struggle of the Afrikaners might not be different from that of the black nationalists.

The idea of internal white colonialism in South Africa detracts from class analysis and can obscure the supreme importance of imperialism in contemporary Africa. Colonialism is a historically-determined mode of political and economic domination. Its method of extraction of economic value is basically extraeconomic. This definitely does not fit South Africa, where capitalism has long entered its imperialist or monopoly stage. South Africa does not thrive by exchange value but rather by *surplus value*. This implies a definite social relationship between black labor and white capital which is not affected by any colonial anachronism in the South African society.

In determining claims about whose country South Africa is, we can only get caught up in the morass of racial classification and pedigree which is the precise ideological recipe of the South African government. Needless to say, this is being fought fiercely by black South Africans and a small white minority. It is also tempting to start talking glibly about "black or African nationalism." First of all, the concept of "black" has changed significantly in South Africa. In the 1950s and 1960s the social divisions betwen Africans, Coloureds, and Asians more or less held, except among some petit-bourgeois intellectuals who belonged to the various liberation movements. However, from the 1970s onwards, starting with the youth movement that culminated in the Soweto uprising, the amalgamation of non-white trade unions, the rise of the United Democratic Front (UDF), and the rejection of the second chamber for Coloureds and Asians in South African parliament, such divisions have been irreversibly shattered. In the current vernacular, terms such as "Coloureds" and "Asians" have been expunged. People refer to themselves as "blacks." But, noticeably, "black" is not yet used interchangeably with "African" except by those blacks who have always called themselves "Africans." Does this signify anything important or is it merely a passing phase? This brings us directly to the national question in South Africa.

THE NATIONAL QUESTION

Classical theories about what a nation is are derived from particular universal languages which are quickly becoming antiquated. For instance, different waves of South Africans have occupied the same territory for up to 500 years, the latest immigrants being the British and Indians who arrived about 150 years ago. They do not have a common language but instead have five major languages in common, all of them spoken to varying degrees. This phenomenon is most marked in the urban areas and is independent of formal education. This means that even with increasing urbanization and industrialization South African cannot hope to dispense with a plurality of languages. Boundaries between linguistic categories in South Africa have always been more fluid than legally-enforced boundaries between racial groups. The attempt to segregate people according to linguistic category in the urban areas has failed, as is illustrated by the rise of integrated popular movements in the last decade.

The Bantustan policy might have partially succeeded in isolating people from one another, as is evidenced by the formation of tribal organizations such as the *Inkatha*. However, there is no evidence that this affected language use. If anything, opposition from the youth to Chief Gatsha Buthelezi and his *Inkatha* cuts across language categories. The Bantustans could not have overcome the problem of linguistic confluence in South Africa. For instance, the people in the Transkei and the Ciskei speak Xhosa as well as English. Knowledge of Afrikaans is also fairly widespread. The northern Bantustans speak northern Sotho, English, and Afrikaans. Basotho Qwa Qwa speaks southern Sotho as does Lesotho and the bordering parts of the Transkei. Likewise, it shares Xhosa with the Transkei and, finally, English with all its neighbors. If language is the medium for cultural representations, then linguistic promiscuity in South Africa is no doubt felicitous. Different cultural codes are understood and, though not used all the time, are invoked in the right circumstances.

Culturally, the difference between a penis-sheath and a pair of trousers might seem dramatic and yet migrant miners have for years moved from one to the other with perfect ease. Likewise in the age of "Native" or "Bantu" commissioners in South Africa, we witnessed whites engaged in traditional ceremonies with full African regalia befitting their status as "supreme chief of the Natives." Whereas in the nineteenth century there was hardly and difference in mode of production, dietary habits, and belief in witchcraft and diviners between Africans and Afrikaners on the highveld; in the twentieth, cultural differences between middle-class English-speakers and missionary-trained African petit-bourgeois elites were only a matter of degree. Of course, the statutory prohibition of mixed marriage was the major barrier. Among African peoples where such prohibitions did not exist, intermarriage, especially in the urban areas, had led to a veritable cultural fusion, a vibrant complex. Tribal stereotypes exist but they are no more than the joking relationships encountered by the ethnographer of Rooiyard in Johannesburg in the 1940s or the stereotypes about the Irish and the Scots in the United Kingdom. The so-called tribal faction fights in the mines especially are more a result of the ghetto mentality fostered by the South African government and the mine owners than a reflection of deep-seated tribal antagonisms. Of course, it is not unusual for certain groups to be used as scapegoats under conditions of severe competition. The inevitable conclusion we reach in this analysis is that in South Africa there is a dynamic, cultural melange which is completely at variance with the government's apartheid policy.

Consequently, one is puzzled and at the same time embarrassed to acknowledge that the position of the South African Communist party on the question of "nationalities," though inspired by a liberatory ideology, coincides with that of the government on Bantustans. Fortunately, one does not have to strain to establish this point because the Communist Party has more publications on this issue than any other political organization in South Africa. From its inception, the Communist Party had been guided by Stalin's thesis on the right of nations to self-determination and the recommendations of the Third International/Comintern to fraternal organizations. As was observed earlier, both of these represented universal texts that had to be translated into the vernacular. The slogan recommended for South Africa in the 1920s was a "Native Republic" which was to fight for the overthrow of British and Afrikaner imperialism and for the restoration of lost territory to the natives. As a further development, in 1932 the Comintern advised that the concept be made more explicit by including the following slogans: "Drive out the imperialists. Complete and immediate national independence for the people of South Africa. For the right of the Zulu, Basuto, etc., nations to form their own independent republics. For the voluntary uniting of the African nations in a Federation of Independent Native Republics." (Compare this to Botha's "constellation of independent nations" in South Africa.)

The Communist Party of South Africa still abides by the same principles, as is witnessed by its program: "Communists recognize the right of all peoples and national groups to self-determination. They respect the languages and progressive traditions of all African peoples, and their right to independent development of their culture." These are noble principles, but to whom do they refer? The Sotho, the Xhosa, the Zulu, the Coloureds, and perhaps the Indians—all of whom the program describes merely as a "community?" All this received wisdom violates the empirical history of South Africa which is being made right in front of our eyes by the people themselves. One can hazard the prediction that in another few years nobody will want to be called "Coloured" in South Africa. Even if some old diehards wished it, how could the so-called Coloureds, who have never had an independent territory, language, and culture, be cast in the frame of a nation? They have always been South Africans, if underprivileged like all other blacks (or is it browns?).

Another way of judging the same issue would be to look at the rise of national organizations and their self-identification. What we have seen since 1912 is Africans projecting themselves as "Africans" and not as representatives of separate "nationalities" or "national groups." Chosen names such as the African National Congress, the All African Convention, the African Youth League, the Society of Young Africa, the Cape African Teachers' Association, and the Pan-Africanist Congress emphasize this self-perception. They also epitomize an aspiration for a transcendent nationhood. This is what has been referred to as African nationalism. On the surface, there is nothing peculiar about it; it occurred everywhere in colonial Africa. Its aim was to overthrow an alien power. It was not until Zimbabwe's (then Rhodesia) struggle to overthrow a "white minority regime" that certain ambiguities began to creep in. This struggle gave significance to the principle of "majority rule" but not necessarily to the principle of "independence," as was the case in the rest of Africa. Had not Rhodesia in the meantime achieved "independence" from Britain? It would have been bad propaganda for the African liberation movement to admit so. All the same, the Zimbabwean freedom-fighters were as preoccupied with the "white settler government" as they were with the "white minority regime." Did this make black nationalists of them? That is a question they must answer themselves.

Of relevance to us is that these ambiguities have plagued the South African struggle. As has been shown, the Africans in South Africa are, and have always been since the turn of the century, committed to African nationalism and to one African nationhood. In that respect, all the national movements are violently opposed to the policy of Bantustans and uphold the integrity of the South African state—but not the South African government. This concept of "independence" does not feature in their political repertoire. Instead, they call for a "non-racial democracy. Is this a tacit acknowledgement that South Africa is already an independent country? This is one instance where the theory of internal "colonialism" runs into difficulties. The acceptance of an existing state and the demand for a "national democracy" which includes the supposed white "colonialists" is a contradiction in terms.

Imperialists and colonialists are worth driving out, as the Comintern had recommended in the 1930s. It has proved hard enough in independent Zimbabwe to reconcile the interests of the black majority with those of the white settlers. How much more difficult would it be with the white "colonialists" in South Africa, if that is what they be?

It has been argued by the followers of the CPSA in the pages of the *African Communist* that

> the great disadvantage of the one-nation thesis is . . . that it obscures the colonial nature of our society and in consequence the national character of our liberation struggle. It is this flaw that the two nations thesis is deliberately designed to counter. . . . This holds essentially that South Africa is a colonial situation of a special type in which two nations, an oppressing nation and an oppressed nation, live side by side within the same territory.

This formulation is certainly unsatisfactory. First, the "colonial nature" of a society is determined by particular political and economic relations, the most critical being domination of pre-capitalist formations by a capitalist one and extraction of value by largely extra-economic means. Not only has South Africa long passed that stage but, historically, it was not peculiar to her. Nor was it contingent on racial oppression. Both the United States and Australia (and the Cape, as is shown by the Great Trek) were *white* colonies of Britain and suffered the same ravages as everybody else (the brutalization of the British ex-convicts in Australia was particularly bad and carried out by British settlers). What is peculiar then about South Africa and former Rhodesia is *racial oppression* in an age of modern imperialism.

It was remarked earlier that all South Africans, irrespective of nationality or physical appearance, are being drawn towards one another, especially in the urban areas. The driving force behind this is undoubtedly the development of commodity and labor relations under capitalism. What has militated against fuller integration is racial oppression and segregation—in a word, *apartheid*. Apartheid created group feelings on either side of the color line. This is what it was meant to do for the whites. Dynamically, as resentment and frustration mounted, it also fostered an increasing sense of solidarity among non-whites. For a while the government succeeded in keeping integration down by practicing territorial segregation among the various groups, even in the urban areas. As is shown by the current upheavals in almost all South African towns, that ploy has lost its ideological efficacy. Under conditions of a continuing crisis, segregation is beginning to wear thin among the whites as well. Emerging class differences among them, as will be argued in the next section, are calling for new ideological projections. In contrast, the blacks who had been kept within narrow confines by the apartheid policy have experience less class differentiation and their aspirant petit-bourgeoisie has not been able to graduate out of the struggle.

Acknowledgement of the fact that there is, and has been, racial oppression in South Africa and that there is group feeling and consciousness on either side of the color line should not be seen as a vindication of the "two-nation" theorists. If South Africa is a capitalist state (as we have reason to believe), then the white racists could not have hoped to form a nation by themselves to the exclusion of the blacks, who constitute more than 70 percent of their labor force. In fact, their policy of racial oppression or apartheid was designed deliberately to guarantee a supply of cheap, servile, black labor. Every communist knows that but every communist is not free of racial indoctrination. On the other hand, the disenfranchised blacks could not have hoped to form a nation without state power and control over national resources. Therefore, political and economic disenfranchisement is what their fight is about. This does not say what they will do once they have got the franchise. "Non-racial democracy" is the common denominator. This is a demand for inclusion in the body policy of the country and guarantees the national integration that has hitherto been frustrated by apartheid. It is noteworthy that since the end of the wars of con- quest in the last quarter of the nineteenth century, the blacks had reconciled themselves to the idea of living in the same territory as the whites. Nevertheless, since the formation of the Union of South Africa in 1910, they have known nothing else but rejection and humiliation from the whites. However, South Africa has not been a contested territory since the end of the 19th century. What has been at issue is hegemonic power *within* it.

To summarize:
a. in South Africa, where territory is not contested either from outside (colonialism) or from inside (secessionism), the concept of "independence" as evolved elsewhere in Africa is inapplicable;
b. South Africa seems not to have a "settler problem" and hence no serious reference has been made to it by the national liberation movements since World War II;
c. consequently, it seems that the idea of "internal colonialism" is a misconception both difficult to sustain logically and

difficult to reconcile with South Africa being a capitalist and not a colonial state;

d. "majority rule" in South Africa, as in Zimbabwe, is perfectly consistent with the concept of a "non-racial" democracy, but does not in itself say anything about socialism;

e. "black nationalism/consciousness" is a reaction to racial discrimination and white chauvinism in South Africa. It is not a political bid to establish an independent nation or state in the same way that African nationalism did elsewhere in Africa. It is a move to create a more inclusive state in which the processes of national integration which have already taken place despite apartheid can continue unimpeded; and

f. finally, this vitiates any suppositions about the right of "nations" to self-determination in South Africa (or in Zimbabwe for that matter).

THE SOUTH AFRICAN STATE: ITS NATURE AND EVOLUTION

It is apparent from our previous discussion that the South African state is a state without a nation. Consequently, every political movement in the country can afford nationalist pretensions. It is interesting that all the South African movements have in their propaganda and programs an everlasting refrain, "our country." The only group for which we have no record of the same is the English-speaking bourgeoisie, starting from the Liberal party through the Progressive party to the present Progressive Federal party. Consistently (and symbolically enough), they refer to South Africa as "this country." Both unconscious reflexes are intriguing. It might be that to some minds South Africa is a contested territory and a base for operations as good as any other. This should not be thought of as a purely moral question. It is apparent that the transnationalization of classes under monopoly capitalism is very uneven. Above all, the vicissitudes of a state without a nation deserve serious attention, as the phenomenon is not peculiar only to South Africa but to virtually all the states in black Africa. The comparison might strike some as odd and undesirable. But racialism, important as it is, might obscure what is otherwise more basic and general. We are accustomed, especially on the left, to hearing certain standard formulae such as "the state is an instrument for class oppression," "the state in a capitalist society at all times serves the interests of the bourgeoisie," and so on. If things were as self-evident as they are made to sound, we would not be able to justify ourselves as a community of social scientists and we would be reduced to being mere consumers of received knowledge. States born under imperialism abound in ambiguities. This is accounted for by the inchoate nature of social classes in imperialist-dominated societies. This in turn, renders the national democratic revolution too difficult to define in terms of its class content.

The conquest of African societies in South Africa was carried out by both the Boers (later Afrikaners) and the British for different reasons. Having escaped from British colonialism in the Cape, the Boers were looking for a free territory to settle. There was vacant land but no free territory. Whatever territory they traversed or coveted turned out to be the domain of one African national group or another. Because they would not accept the authority of these groups as any supplicant group was expected to, the Boers had to live by the gun which ultimately delivered to them the Boer Republics of The Orange Free State and the Transvaal. It was here that they carved out big estates (averaging 3,000 morgen each) for themselves and set up independent administrations. But they had neither labor nor capital. For the former, they turned to the vanquished Africans whom they used as labor-tenants. (There was forced labor as well, but fear of British intervention kept it in check.) This did not really compensate for lack of capital and managerial skills among the Afrikaner landowners. Rent-paying African squatters became the solution to that problem. Africans farmed for the landowners, using their own farming equipment and seeds, in exchange for an agreed amount of land for their private use. This was prevalent during the latter half of the 19th century and was referred to as "kaffir farming." If labor-tenant relations (and rentier-landlords) were the nearest thing to feudalism we have ever had in South Africa, it did not last long. It was closely followed by commodity relations, of which the dispossessed Africans were the leading agents from the 1860s to 1913.

In contrast to the Boers, who still aspired to being slave-owners or (at least) feudal lords, the British settlers had been brought over to the Cape to produce wool and to Natal to produce sugar for Britain along capitalist lines. The British capitalist state undertook to create the necessary political and social conditions for such production. This meant subjugating all pre-existing political authorities to British rule and creating free labor. Among other things, this meant the abolition of slavery, which was the major cause for the Great Trek. For the Africans it meant complete domination of their subsistence mode of production. The attack was two-pronged—large-scale seizure of land and imposition of several taxes payable in cash. This both created a big reservoir of cheap labor for white employers and eliminated any prospect of surplus production by the Africans in the reserves. This pattern has been repeated only in Zimbabwe, Swaziland, and to some extent in Kenya. Elsewhere in black Africa, the original subsistence sector was allowed to participate in surplus production through cultivation of cash crops, heavily taxed through marketing boards or other extractive mechanisms. Falling real incomes and a finely-tuned system of taxation guaranteed a steady flow of labor—seasonal or otherwise. The incorporation of the African household economy at only the level of social reproduction of labor in South Africa has led to a generalization by the South African analysts about the absolute need on the part of colonial or underdeveloped capitalism for a "reserve army of cheap labor." As will be shown later, this generalization is too sweeping even for South Africa.

The subordination of pre-existing modes of production by colonial capitalism in South Africa was not limited to Africans. The Boer Republics and their erstwhile rentier-landlords also came under fire. The discovery of gold in 1884-85 might have quickened the pace, but there were already complaints from emerging white commercial farmers in the Orange Free State, the Transvaal, and northern Natal about unfair competiton from "cheap kaffir farming." The British colonial administration, which saw prospects for expanding the market and capitalist production in the whole region, listened to these complaints more than sympathetically. Sooner or later the antiquated mode of production in the Boer Republics had to be swept aside to allow for the free flow of capital and labor. The Boers, who by then identified themselves as Africans ("Afrikaners" in their language) disagreed and went to war against the British, whom they described as foreigners (*"uitlanders"*). The obstensible reason given by the Afrikaners for resisting to the bitter end was to defend their sovereignty, which in fact was already "subject to British seizurainty" by previous "agreements" (threats). The British did not pose just a formal threat to the Afrikaners; the threat was real. The question then is: At this historical juncture and in the totality of things, what social force did the Afrikaners represent? An answer to this question is the key to an understanding of the reflexes of the South African state since the unification of 1910.

Many answers to the question have been given and a great deal of new research material has been applied to the issue. The prevalent view is that the Afrikaners most feared domination by British imperial capital. Whether or not the distinction between foreign and "national" capital in South Africa at the turn of the century can be clarified in general, the alleged fear of British capital by the Afrikaners presupposes a few things which might not be true. First, it presupposes that all Afrikaners stood in the same relation to capital. Second, it presupposes that the Afrikaners were owners of national capital and that this capital was incompatible with foreign capital.

According to information at hand, a small section of the Afrikaner landlords had turned to commercial farming by the end of the 19th century. They were, therefore, owners of agricultural capital. But so did a number of city-based foreign companies in The Orange Free State and the Transvaal and the English-speaking farmers in Natal and the Cape. Although the exact ratios have not yet been worked out, one suspects that the non-Afrikaners in fact held a higher ratio of agricultural capital than the Afrikaners at this point in time. Yet, they did not feel threatened by British "foreign" capital. Instead, within the South African economy they were willing to cooperate with it or take advantage of it. This would include those African *bywoners* (share-croppers) who were looking for opportunities for investment in agriculture, free of Afrikaner domination and exploitation. Therefore, objectively and statistically, it cannot be said that at the turn of this century the Afrikaners represented "national" capital per se. Also, it has yet to be proved that whatever agricultural capital they had was incompatible with British capital which was largely in the mining industry (diamonds and gold).

In the last quarter of the 19th century, the majority of the Afrikaners were not capitalists but rather were medium and small producers, generally inefficient, who since the days of slavery in the Cape looked upon farm work as "*kaffir werk.*" Secondly, there was among them a dearth of industrial skills, which in the Cape had been provided by slaves from Malaya and Mauritius. The majority of them were, from every point of view, an extremely rural petit-bourgeoisie. While big capital, agricultural or industrial, cannot be said to have been an immediate threat to them, British *political domination* was. It had two implications for the relatively backward Afrikaner petit-bourgeoisie. First, the British colonial government was quite willing to overrule all forms of unfree labor by which it benefited and for which it relied on the Boer state, whose ideological outlook was a guarantee. As a corollary to this the British administration encouraged commercial farming, which exposed the backward sector to unfair competition even from the blacks. Second, the establishment of British industries under conditions of "free labor" was bound to expose the poorer Afrikaners to competition for jobs with blacks who were not only used to hard work but also had no preconceived ideas about "white" work or wages. Finally, although we have no evidence for it from The Orange Free State and the Transvaal where education for Africans started late, in the Cape the educated petit-bourgeois elite evoked the strongest antipathy from the Afrikaners. They sarcastically referred to individual members of this class as *"swarte Engelsman."* The 1857 Constitution of the Cape, the policy of "exempted Natives," and qualified franchise made the emergence of this class possible and the Afrikaners rightly feared that they would be used against them, politically. It is true that until the abolition of the special vote for Africans in 1936, the enfranchised Africans voted for the English-speaking United Party or independent English-speaking candidates.

It is, therefore, our hypothesis that the overriding fear of the Afrikaners was loss of political control which enabled them to protect what they could not defend under British dominion, and assimilation of black elites and workers. The rise of Afrikaner nationalism in this context becomes explicable. The economistic argument about competition between "foreign" and "national" capital is empirically weak and theoretically unsound. It has been hypothesized by the same people who claim that the development of capitalism in South Africa took the "Prussian Path"—a combination of "maize and gold." This presupposes the existence of common interests between British mining capital and Afrikaner agricultural capital. But was there in fact big Afrikaner capital? If so, why did it fail to overrule its own petit-bourgeoisie (and later workers) and instead join them to fight the British, who unambiguously represented big industrial capital? Acceptance of the "maize and gold" thesis renders inoperable the hypothesis about the struggle between "foreign" and "national" capital. Both obscure the basically political nature of Afrikaner nationalism against the British and against the Africans. The Afrikaners were quite happy to take advantage of British mining capital in South Africa and the African majority as long as they *ruled* both. As far as big capital was concerned, they thus could appropriate surplus allocation as a petit-bourgeoisie without affecting any similar interests among their ranks. In surpressing the African majority, they could count on the support of big capital, which had a vested interest in a ready supply of cheap, *docile* black labor. It is our hunch that both conditions do not apply any longer and, hence, the Afrikaner government, politically beleaguered, is likely to move from bad to worse.

A few illustrations will suffice to show that *politics* had been in command in the struggle of the Afrikaners since their military defeat at the beginning of the century until their final victory in 1948. At the time of Union they insisted on formalized racism to protect the interests of "people of European descent." As is known, big capital was quite willing to embrace "all civilised people" as was the case in the Cape. As is shown by the 1913 Land Act which confined Africans to only 13 percent of the land in the country, both the British and the Afrikaners were agreed on the need for cheap black labor. After all, in crushing the Afrikaner Republics, Lord Milner had declared that one of the objectives of the British government was "a well-regulated supply of labour from the Cape to the Limpopo." The African peasantry which emerged and was extremely competitive up to the time of the passing of the Land Act had to be smashed for the benefit of both British industrial capital and the rural Afrikaner petit-bourgeoisie. Squatting and sharecropping on white farms by Africans was prohibited. Only hired labor was legally permissible. A great many Afrikaners in the *platteland* could not afford commercial farming even with the cheapened black labor. Therefore, they started drifting to the urban areas (especially the Rand) in search of employment. There, they were faced with the same kind of competition they had met from the African *bywoners* (squatters). So, the African workers, like their fellow peasants, had to be defeated not economically but *politically*.

From 1913 onwards white workers, the least skilled of whom— namely, Afrikaners—could not benefit from the usual distinction between artisans and laborers, started fighting for higher white wages so as to maintain a "civilised standard of living." These demands met with approval with Hertzog's National Party as well as from the International Socialist League, from which came the majority of the members of the Communist Party of South Africa. Shortly after its formation in 1921 the CPSA was debating the question of whether or not Africans should be included in the labor movement. When the 1922 white miners' strike erupted, the African workers refused to be left out, showing an impressive demonstration of strength. The CPSA came out in support of the segregationist white workers on the grounds that they were the "core of the proletariat" and that "their success would liberate all the proletariat."

The one white group that was not reconciled to the idea of higher wages for whites which were not commensurate with their labor pro- ductivity was the mine-owners, that is, the big industrial bourgeoisie in South Africa. They prevailed over Smuts' government, which represented their interests. Consequently, the strike was crushed ruthlessly by the army. This fanned the flames of Afrikaner nationalism. The chauvinism of the white workers and their allies issued in a permanently divided working-class. The white workers left the Labour Party for Hertzog's petit-bourgeois National Party and the black workers for the Industrial and Commercial Workers Union of Africa whose, acronym, ICU, got popularized in the vernacular in the Rand as *Kea Kubona*—I See You (White Man). Like the African National Congress in 1913, the ICU was a reaction to political exclusion and its long-term implications. The long-term implications were allocation, and not generation, of surplus. In our view, this is the major distinction between nationalist movements and class or class-based organizations.

The Afrikaners, despite their anti-imperialist rhetoric and flirtation with a misconceived idea of Bolshevism by their laborites, were not opposed to capitalism. Instead, they wanted British capital in South Africa to compensate them for their *economic* weaknesses. Since capitalism does not allocate value according to economic weakness but according to economic strength, the Afrikaners had to find a power base *outside* of economics. The fall of the Smuts government as a sequel to the miners' revolt and the rise to power of the National–Labor Pact under Hertzog in 1924 gave them a glorious opportunity for consolidating an Afrikaner *block* consisting of the Afrikaner petit-bourgeoisie, drawn from both rural and urban areas, and the white urban workers who were not all Afrikaner but identified with the Afrikaner government. This block was opposed to both British domination and African advancement in particular. Its first act after coming into power was to declare a "civilised labour policy," which meant "white worker privilege" and official discrimination against black workers. This was given legal status by the Industrial Conciliation Act of 1924, the Wage Act of 1925, and the Mines and Works Amendment Act of 1926. The Industrial Conciliation Act stripped the African workers, who henceforth were categorized as "employees," of their right to form trade unions and to strike for higher wages. Parallel to this was a conscious effort by the government to reserve most jobs in the service sector—for example, the bureaucracy, the railways, and harbors—for white workers who were commonly Afrikaners.

The South African mining bourgeoisie had been thrown out of its own parliament and the road had been opened to Afrikaner petit-bourgeois economic nationalism. After the First World War there had already been demands from its representatives not only for reallocation of surplus but also for its reinvestment. For instance, in 1918 the Federated Chamber of Industries urged the government to allocate more funds for the development of manufacturing industries. Secondary industries, though penetrated by British capital, were still an open frontier.

But for the Afrikaner petit-bourgeoisie the scope was much wider in agriculture than in industry. It is therefore notable that the 1922

Drought Investigation Committee, while critical of the "bad farming practices" of the Afrikaners, blamed lack of necessary capital for the regressive nature of South African agriculture. The Pact government responded to these demands by reallocating ever-increasing amounts for investment in agriculture and "protected" industries. The latter referred to locally-owned industries, as against the mining industries which operated largely with foreign capital. In 1925 the government not only put a high tariff on imported goods but also revised upwards the price indices for protected industrial goods. In a double strategy it used its protection to induce employers in the relevant industries to use more white labor. In 1933 the Customs Tariff Commission estimated the number of whites employed in protected industries at 26,000–28,000. It concluded that "for 1933 the ratio of employment of Europeans is higher in protected than in economic secondary industry."

The idea of "economic" industries reveals two factors: (a) that the protected industries were not necessarily economic, and (b) that though the issue had been posed as foreign versus "indigenous" capital, in reality the protective policy signaled discrimination in favor of Afrikaner neophyte industrialists and their political allies. The Afrikaner government was not satisfied with simply supporting favored, flagging industries. In 1928 it took the one single step which made a difference economically. This step was the establishment of the Iron and Steel Corporation of South Africa (ISCOR) as a public enterprise. Not only did it lay the foundation for a *national capital goods* sector, but it also inaugurated state capitalism in South Africa, which had far-reaching effects. The immediate effect was that the government had discretionary power over the supply and level of prices of technological inputs for the different sectors of the economy. For instance, consistent with its policy, protected industries and agriculture were highly favored.

It is unusual for agriculture to be favored in a growing economy or an economy which is still going through the stage of primitive accumulation. South Africa might be an instructive exception. From the mid-1920s onwards the Afrikaner government offered generous loans, subsidies, railway concessions, and tax reductions or rebates to white (mostly Afrikaner) farmers. The economic value of these benefits averaged between 13 and 15 percent of the total contribution of the agriculture sector to the country's GNP (the situation has not changed much since). The source of these revenues was the leading sector or the economy, namely, the mines. This can be gleaned from the fact that while the value of gold output increased from a base of 100 in 1913 to 220.9 in 1937 and the dividends declared to 203, in the same period taxation on the mining industry rose from a base of 100 to 1,191. Thus, state taxation as a percentage of total dividends paid was 13.33 percent in 1913 and had risen to 78.28 percent by 1936 (Frankel, 1938).

This was corroborated by evidence, submitted by the Gold Producer's Committee of the Transvaal Chamber of Miners, to the Departmental Committee on Mining Taxation in 1935, which showed that state taxes on gold mining in South Africa were higher than in any country in the capitalist world. For the benefit of the farmers in the backveld, the government also built infrastructure, which was considered uneconomic by its opponents. In addition, far from maintaining the previous quality-regulation measures, the Pact government passed legislation to increase the prices of virtually all domestic agriculture and secondary culminated in the Marketing Act of 1937. It is not as if the mining magnates accepted this with equanimity. The 1940–41 Industrial and Agricultural Requirements Commission could not help pointing out that there were "heavy excess costs both in agriculture and secondary industry" and that these two activities could "exist under present conditions only because of the surpluses diverted to them by means of taxation, price raising measures, subsidies and the like." The Afrikaner government had *politically* overruled and constrained big business to serve its largely petit-bourgeois interests.

This is perfectly consistent, for it is said that "the state serves the interests of the ruling class." But according to the same doctrine, the petit-bourgeoisie is a vacillating class incapable of an independent political enterprise. Secondly, by virtue of its position, it is incapable of producing real (added) value in the manner of the capitalists and the workers. It can, therefore, only benefit by extraction of surplus value by the capitalist class. This is heady universal language and requires translation into the vernacular. The Afrikaners succeeded eminently in their political enterprise and in their strategy to use state capitalism to compensate for their economic weakness. Nobody who has suffered under Afrikaner state oppression and that of the other petit-bourgeois governments in most of the Third World countries would deny the former. It is, therefore, our hypothesis that the petit-bourgeoisie is capable of a successful political enterprise, depending on the objective strength of the contending classes. But this qualifier is true of all classes.

For that matter, the term "independent" in classical texts is misleading for even in the European bourgeois revolution, the leading class (the bourgeoisie) needed the support of all oppressed classes. The success of the national democratic revolution in ex-colonial countries is predicated on this premise, whether the struggle is socialist-oriented or not. In their struggles, the Communist parties of China and Viet Nam relied heavily on the support of the peasants and other progressive sections of the petit-bourgeoisie. This gives prominence to the leading role of the petit-bourgeoisie in underdeveloped countries. It is, therefore, our second hypothesis that all nationalist/national movements in underdeveloped countries are most likely to be dominated by the interests of the petit-bourgeoisie. While the existence of a progressive petit-bourgeoisie in these countries cannot be denied or dismissed, it cannot be used as an index of a socialist struggle. It is by historical necessity a minority force in competition for the support of the workers and peasants who under conditions of nationalism mistake their interests for those of the leading class.

In the short run this illusion might be confirmed by the protective or concessionary policies of a petit-bourgeois government fighting for survival under conditions of imperialism, as happened in South Africa under the Afrikaners and might happen again under black nationalists. Further, this is not contingent on private ownership of the means of production but on effective control over the means of production, as under state capitalism. Accordingly, it is our contention that under modern conditions *control* over means of production can be as effective as ownership was under classical capitalism. This gives the petit-bourgeoisie opportunities that did not exist before. It is also a strong warning against equating state capitalism with socialization of the means of production. The bureaucratic petit-bourgeois elite is quite capable of expropriating the direct producers, as is attested by many known cases.

THE SOUTH AFRICAN STATE: ITS REVOLUTIONS AND PROSPECTS FOR THE FUTURE

Nor does the story end there. The problem of the state petit-bourgeoisie, unlike the bourgeoisie and the proletariat, is that it cannot reproduce itself consistently and, therefore, indefinitely. South Africa is a supreme example of this. The Afrikaner petit-bourgeoisie, appreciative of its military defeat by the British bourgeoisie, mobilized disadvantaged Afrikaners of all classes and other disgruntled whites, politically. Upon success, it adopted a policy of protectionism and economic nationalism for the benefit of its constituency and thus forsook any pretense of being representative of "all classes." Through these policies, successive Afrikaner governments up to the 1950s were able to satisfy both their bought working-class and forested businessmen and farmers. In the process it spawned, unwittingly, a true Afrikaner bourgeoisie.[1] While the agricultural bourgeoisie had made its appearance in the 1930s, the industrial bourgeoisie appeared in the 1960s. They accepted apartheid but had some reservations about the policy of Bantustans.

This had alredy been foreshadowed by the report of the government-appointed Tomlinson Commission in 1955. The Commission had recommeded that the black industrial workers be accepted as an integral part of the urban population in South Africa. It further acknowledged that the African "reserves" were overpopulated by two-thirds. It accordingly recommended that the surplus population be moved to create room for yeoman farming among the rural Africans. This was the voice of capital speaking and it coincided with that of the English-speaking bourgeoisie. It was instantly rejected by Verwoerd's government. But the internal struggle between the old Afrikaner petit-bourgeois leadership and its foster-child, the new Afrikaner bourgeoisie, had begun. The latter also had its intellectual wing, as is shown by the symptomatic revolt of a number of Afrikaner professors, literati, and clergymen against the doctrinaire *Broederbond* in particular from the late 1950s onwards.

The economic boom of the 1960s had not only raised the capitalist stakes but had also increased the demand for skilled labor. Advancement of black workers became a necessity, vindicating the position of the bourgeoisie in general. Ironically enough, when the recession set in in the 1970s resulting in unofficial strikes among the black workers, it added extra weight to the arguments of "enlightened" capitalist who urged abandonment of the olds ways in favor of stability and productivity. As the political and economic crisis deepened in the 1970s, the schism between the conservative (*verkrampte*) wing of the Afrikaners representing petit-bourgeois and privileged white worker interests, and the enlightened (*verlighte*) wing representing the interests of the emergent Afrikaner bourgeoisie, got so acute that it led to the dramatic split between the *Nasionale Party* and the *Herstigte Nasionale Party*. Although one would have thought that the position of the national bourgeoisie would have given them respite, actual events from the 1976 uprising to the current upheavals belie this. As was mentioned in the introduction, militancy and solidarity among the black popular masses has increased. Under these conditions, Botha's like Vorster's *verlighte* government cannot fulfill its historic mission, that is, the transformation of petit-bourgeois Afrikanerdom. It is caught on the horns of a dilemma.

With the worsening political turmoil in South Africa, the dramatic recession in the economy, and threatened economic sanctions, the national bourgeiosie is urging ameliorative intervention. The government, predominantely *verlighte*, is anxious to meet these calls as is shown by its ill-fated Second Chamber for Coloureds and its kite-flying on possible retreat on the question of Bantustans and on "power sharing" between white and black. But, in fact, it is torn between the convergent interests of the Afrikaner and English-speaking bourgeoisie on the one hand and the demands of the enfranchised white petit-bourgeoisie and workers on whom it has always depended for votes and security on the other hand. The latter, fearing for their interests which had been racially defined and protected since the Act of Union in 1910, are bracing themselves to fight a rear-guard battle. In this they seem to have the unannounced support of both the military and the civilian wings of the white bureaucracy. This is unheard of in the history of South Africa. In the traditionally formalistic setup in the country, the bureaucracy had remained unimportant as a political force taking its cues from the executive. This is a further crack in the Afrikaner power block, whose implications have not yet been fully analyzed. But certainly the advancing struggle by the disenfranchised black population increases its importance and appeals to the *kragdadige* (zeal) mentality of the right wing.

Therefore, each concession or reform the government makes to placate the blacks is seen as weakness, if not betrayal. This effectively puts the *verlighte* government on the defensive. Nothing demonstrates this more clearly than Botha's scandalous retreat in his much-heralded speech to the National Convention of his Party in August, 1985. After consultations with his international allies and briefings with some of his black neighbors, it was agreed that he renounce apartheid, offer the blacks some power-sharing, subject to negotiation, and scrap the policy of Bantustans. As is known, at the crucial moment, he ultimately reverted to the *kragdadige* language: "We shall not be dictated to by foreigners." The cat was already out of the bag and the leader of the *verkramptes*, Treunicht, lost no time in chastising Botha for his ineptness and idle talk about the *Bantoes* "who spend their time thinking about sex." Even though the BBC interviewer was too embarrassed to pursue the point, this is the vernacular in which Afrikanerdom was conceived in history and in ideology.

As of now, petit-bourgeois Afrikanerdom has suffered its ultimate demise. Its heir-apparent by history is beleaguered. It is faced with irreconcilable antagonisms: white petit-bourgeois and worker privilege and black mass deprivation. Militancy on both sides diminishes the chances of the *verlighte* government fulfilling its historic mission, namely, the re-institution of bourgeois political rule. If the Union of

South Africa in 1910 had marked the unification of the Afrikaner agrarian bourgeoisie and the British industrial bourgeoisie, the so-called "union of maize and gold," the present polarization would not have occurred except along *class*—and not racial—lines. For the bourgeoisie, the complete domination of the African traditional mode of subsistence was sufficient guarantee of an unlimited supply of black labor and a potentially large domestic market, something still not given to South Africa. As is illustrated by their political revolt and ensuing economic nationalism, this would not have allayed the fears of the Afrikaner petit-bourgeoisie and workers who felt sandwiched between British imperialism and the African multitudes, *die swarte gevaar* (which does not exactly give one the impression of idle fornicators).

Furthermore, if the union of the bourgeoisie had been a fact, one of its consequences would have been the birth of a truly national bourgeoisie in alliance with international capitalism in the same way as the present *verlighte* Afrikaner bourgeoisie is. This would have pre-empted the rise of Afriakner nationalism and blunted African proto-nationalism, since it would not have been averse to African petit-bourgeois aspirations, as is historically true of all national bourgeoisie(s). Class differentiation would have been the primary thing. This would have been consonant with the dynamic of a bourgeois national democratic revolution in the classical sense. We would not have referred to it as nationalism precisely because of its all-embracing nature. Heretical as it may sound, nationalism is by nature *sectarian*. It is either a reaction to exclusion or a claim to exclusiveness—an affirmation of a particularistic identity. It may lead to the establishment of a nation or its opposite, secession. At a certain point all these become a matter of definition, as is shown by the history of most African states since the anti-colonial struggle began.

Of immediate relevance to us is nationalism in South Africa. Most analysts would agree that in South Africa the national democratic revolution was emptied of its bourgeois meaning by the exclusion from the beginning of black South Africans of all classes. In that context, Afrikaner nationalism since its inception in the 1920s could not have been, short of secession, anything but a perversion of the idea of a nation. Confirmation of this is found in the belated attempt by the *verlighte* Afrikaners to redefine their concept of a nation, and thus, reaffirming the original notion of "all civilized people" espoused by the liberal British bourgeoisie. In contrast, African/black nationalism as a reaction to exclusion has tended to be inclusive in its orientation, as shown by the general slogan, "non-racial democracy." Insofar as this is true and contrary to its popular rhetoric, it *does not* represent a nation in and by itself, as happened elsewhere in Africa (barring Zimbabwe). If successful in its objective, it would not have of necessity transcended the original South African bourgeois idea of a nation, consisting of "all civilized people" and a "well-regulated supply of labor" (that is, effective incorporation of all into the capitalist system).

Marxists within the South African liberation movement are acutely aware of the implications of the above fact. While there is unanimity on the question of the struggle for the extension of democratic rights to all, "irrespective of colour, creed or sex," there is no agreement on the nature of the national democratic revolution. Some, such as the members of the Communist party, advocate a two-stage theory—a national democratic (bourgeois ?) revolution followed by a socialist revolution. In the first stage, the right of the African majority "which is the most oppressed and exploited" are given primacy, whereas the belief in the second stage is based on the existence of a "vast proletariat" in South Africa whose majority also happens to be "African." There is general equivocation on the role of the white working class, as there has always been. Meanwhile, lack of a necessary link between the first and second stages in light of a divided working class has prompted some, especially the members of the Unity Movement, to vehemently oppose the two-stage theory. Their counter-argument is that "in the morrow of the so-called national democratic revolution" the African peasants and workers will find themselves begging and will, therefore, be obliged to continue the struggle. The overtones of a permanent revolution are implicit in the second position. But the grounds for supposing that a socialist revolution is implicit in the South African national liberation struggle are as tenuous as the postulated link between the national democratic and the socialist revolution in the two-stage theory.

Our suspicion (confirmed by prior knowledge) is that both positions are largely a rendering of universal texts, not filtered through local history, whatever the theoretical implications might be. While the general postulates of the New Democracy, one of which concerns the foreclosure of the development of an independent national bourgeoisie in ex-colonial countries since the rise of imperialism, are an important starting-point for a theory of revolution in underdeveloped countries; their prescriptive value is always subject to question. Putting aside the question of whether or not countries such as South Africa (or Zimbabwe for that matter) have had a national bourgeoisie, it is obvious that the New Democracy theorists, like classical Marxists, underestimated the capacity of the petit-bourgeoisie in new states to mount their own political enterprise and frustrate any attempts towards a socialist transformation. Africa is full of examples as a sequel to African nationalism.

Then the question is, why would the South African black petit-bourgeoisie not follow suit? Further, any concessions that will be made by the white bourgeoisie and imperialism will be directed towards them as before. Already, they are being courted by those who seek a negotiated settlement in South Africa. It is the obduracy of the Afrikaners that is fouling up the whole affair. For the would-be socialists, this is made even worse by the existence of a divided working class in South Africa. While they may wish otherwise, we know that, objectively, the white workers in South Africa, as in former Rhodesia, are the backbone of the army and the security forces. Under the present conditions, there is not even a chance of their "turning their guns against their class enemy." Does this necessarily commit the liberation struggle in South Africa to a bourgeois solution, as has been suggested by the two-stage theorists? If not, what is the meaning of the often-repeated slogan of "national democratic revolution?"

Here, theoretical and strategic questions often get confused. The first theoretical supposition is that the national democratic revolution is a necessary condition for a socialist revolution. At the same time and consistent with the postulates of the "New Democracy," it is admitted that under conditions of monopoly capitalism, imperialism will abort the national democratic revolution by imposing a petit-bourgeois comprador class whose interests will be opposed to those of the majority of the people. Despite this acknowledgement, it is argued that strategically it would be a mistake for the workers to come out with a socialist program at this stage of the revolution for they would alienate the other classes, namely, the black petit-bourgeoisie and white liberals whose support they need. This is pure cant. If the chances for a democratic revolution are foreclosed under imperialism, why would it hurt more for the workers and the peasants to insist on their class interests now rather than later? Second, why should it be supposed that in the interim period the petit-bourgeoisie can dispense with the support of the popular classes? There is no record of this in all the recent nationalist struggles. Besides, under the "New Democracy" the slogan is: "If the workers and the peasants be weak, the petit-bourgeoisie will betray."

Accordingly, it is in the interests of the workers and the peasants, both in the short run and in the long run, to prevail over the black nationalist petit-bourgeoisie. As for the white liberals and other interested parties, the onus rests on them. The point is, while the support of all progressive forces is welcome, anything that threatens the conditions of livelihood of the majority of the people should be strenuously resisted. What this means in practice or what program it envisages has been a source of controversy in the past. The main reason has been misapplication of historical materialism by some Marxists. First, the tendency to treat "socialism" as a finite stage with a beginning and an end is contrary to Marxism. Far from being a mode of production, socialism is a transitional stage whose content is determined by concrete class struggles at a given time. In the process, historical experience tells us what form the primary contradiction between capital and labor is most likely to assume. This is not a problem of necessary conditions, but of prevailing objective conditions—that is, dialectical and not derivative.

In the case of South Africa it is already clear what will threaten the conditions of livelihood of the majority of the people. First among these is an imposed settlement as in Zimbabwe. While theorists such as Samir Amin might advocate "de-linking" and express fears about "re-compradorization," it is doubtful if any of this is relevant to southern Africa. So far, South Africa has not given the blacks in the region even the chance to be "compradors." Instead, she has sought to reduce all the neighboring states to Bantustans. So, the would-be compradors in the region are embattled and the struggle continues despite their so-called independence. Therefore, the actual danger is that if a negotiated settlement is achieved in South Africa itself, a virgin black comprador class will come into existence for the first time in the region—which might be a boon to imperialism which is having the problem of propping up jaded compradors in Asia and Latin America. By engaging in a sustained struggle against imperialism and capitalist exploitation, the people in southern Africa have in fact "de-linked." The real question is whether they allow their aspirant petit-bourgeoisie to "re-link."

Already, there are a number of pitfalls in the existing programs of demand. The slogan, "land to the tillers," interpreted as a bourgeois right, might mean that the landless African peasantry which was forced into labor migration from the late nineteenth century onwards will never be able to lay claim to the 87 percent of the land that was taken away from them during colonial conquest. Not surprisingly, this is consistent with the position of the South African communists who believe that, anyway, there is no black peasantry in South Africa. In that case it would be the democratic right of the whites to hold whatever land they happen to occupy. Another example is the open declaration that the people shall share in the mineral and industrial wealth of the country, without specifying how. Nationalization policies and state capitalism can no longer be treated as progressive measures without relating them to the question of balance of power between contending classes in the transitional period.

Experience has shown that if the direct producers do not hold the balance of power in any alliance of classes, they are liable to political and economic expropriation by the petit-bourgeois bureaucratic elite. If in formulating programs for revolutionary transformation we are guided by strict historical analysis, we cannot but conclude that in the imperialist epoch the workers and the peasants can only guarantee the conditions of their livelihood and social reproduction by stamping the revolution with their own image and, thus, prevail over the petit-bourgeoisie and forestall its likely deviations. This in itself and by itself is not tantamount to a class program but merely puts primacy on the interests of the exploited and dominated majority, without which we cannot meaningfully talk of democracy.

Socialst democracy is on the agenda precisely because of the unrealizability of bourgeois democracy under conditions of imperialism and monopoly capitalism. These are the objective conditions under which all contemporary liberation struggles are being conducted. Therefore, the question of whether South Africa is on the verge of a bourgeois revolution, or something else, is most pertinent.

NOTE

1. Founding Afrikaner leaders such as Louis Botha might have been big landowners, but there is no evidence that they were *big capitalists*. Likewise, W.A. Hofmeyr's insurance companies, SANTAM and SANLAM—whose capital stocks stood at a meagre £20,000 in 1918 and would have been ruined in 1922 if it had not been for a loan of £50,000 from the Standard Bank when The Orange Free State Chamber of Executors (in which 60 percent of SANLAM capital was invested) was liquidated—cannot be cited as examples of Afrikaner finance-capital in the pre–World War II period. Therefore, those who wish to argue otherwise will have to produce the necessary statistical evidence instead of being guided by surface impressions. Moreover, individual cases do not make a class. Likewise, not all capitalists are part of the bourgeoisie in the sense of control of the commanding heights of the national economy.

3

The Political Economy of the South African Revolution

Bernard Magubane

The white man in the South African Colonies feels that the colony ought to be his and kept up for him, because he, perhaps, with his life in his hand, went forth as a pioneer to spread the civilization of Europe and to cultivate the wilds of the world's surface. If he has not done so himself, his father did it before him, and he thinks that the gratitude of the Mother Country should maintain for him the complete ascendency which his superiority to the black man has given him. I feel confident that he will maintain his own ascendency, and think that the Mother Country should take care that the ascendency be not too complete.

Anthony Trollope

PRELIMINARY REMARKS

The study of South Africa continues to pose a dilemma to the social scientist. Insofar as it owes its present circumstances to the postfeudal movement from northwestern Europe, the movement that "discovered" North and South America, Australia, and the sea route to India, South Africa is part of the so-called New World.

However, unlike the United States, Canada, Australia, and New Zealand, that is, countries that the Europeans claim as part of the West, South Africa remains an African country and therefore part of the Third World. What makes South Africa the country of the African is not the fact that blacks constitute the majority of the population nor even that they are the indigenous inhabitants. After all, remnants of the indigenous peoples of America, Australia, and New Zealand are still there, but clearly their lands, except for the reservations to which they have been confined, no longer belong to them; more they are clearly fugitives in their native countries. That is, they have been reduced to anthropological museums in which researchers continue to indulge their nostalgia about "primitive" cultures.[1]

What makes South Africa the black man's country is that after almost three centuries of unrelenting warfare by European settlers to exterminate him and to reduce him to a fugitive and marginal status, the African today occupies the very heart of the South African society as its worker.[2] This unenviable position the African occupies has only one consolation for him, and that is, he holds in his hands the fate of South Africa. In other words, despite all the suffering he has borne, despite all the tribulations that are still to come his way, the African nonetheless determines and will continue to determine the future history of South Africa. The current attempts to denationalize him from what is called "White South Africa" notwithstanding, South Africa is a black man's country. This single fact separates the fate of Native Americans, Australians, Canadians, and New Zealanders from that of Native South Africans, despite the obvious superiority in their material conditions at the present moment.[3]

SOUTH AFRICA: THE KEY QUESTION

The crucial question that confronts social scientists today is: Why did the black people of South Africa not suffer the fate of other peoples in what are called white settler colonies? Alternatively, what are the implications of the fact that even though white settlers claim the country to be their own, Africans in South Africa constitute the majority of the population in every part of South Africa? In other words, how should the African struggle be conceptualized?

The white rulers of South Africa have tried to deal with this dilemma at two levels. First, the Nationalist party that has ruled South Africa since 1948 has waged an ideological war by manufacturing a version of past and present South Africa which they have systematically attempted to impose everywhere from the schoolroom to international public opinion. According to this fiction, when the Dutch settlers arrived at the Cape in 1652 they found a country that was virtually empty. They penetrated to the interior peacefully until they met other intruders who were migrating south from the north. These intruders are depicted as the epitome of savage barbarians without culture, achievements, or history, who waged aggressive wars and raids against the innocent settlers. With a bible in one hand and a rifle in the other, the settlers fought to achieve victory over these savages. The impression is given that African settlements were always more or less confined to the areas that in 1913 were set aside as reservations. Secondly, the white rulers have physically moved "excess" Africans from the so-called white areas to the reservations where they can pursue their "own" modes of development without interference, just as whites pursue their cultural development without interference. Were this version of South African history without consequence it would be laughed at and dismissed as nonsense. Unfortunately, it tells a great deal about the character of white settler society.

White settlers became the historic instruments created by the emerging world economy of capitalism in the seventeenth century to establish beachheads in certain key areas of the world that were being incorporated. The white settler would safeguard colonial conquest and secure these countries as future outlets for excess population and for investment of capital from the metropolitan country. Anthony Trollope, a British novelist who visited South Africa in the 1870s, in his influential book *South Africa*, revealed a basic aspect of the imperial frame of mind: the belief that the possession of the virtues of responsibility, trust, and integrity were the preserve of the English and that these virtues legitimized intervention and the seizing of power over the so-called "backward" peoples of the earth:

> Of all the questions which a conscientious man has ever had to decide, this is one of the most difficult. The land clearly belongs to the inhabitants of it—by as good a title as England belongs to the English or Holland to the Dutch. But the advantage of spreading population is so manifest, and the necessity of doing so has so clearly been indicated to us by nature, that no man, let him be ever so conscientious, will say that throngs of human beings from the overpopulated civilized countries should refrain from spreading themselves over unoccupied countries partially occupied by savage races. Such a doctrine would be monstrous, and could be held only by a fanatic in morality. And yet there always comes a crisis in which the stronger, the more civilized,

and the Christian race is called upon to inflict a terrible injustice on the unoffending owner of the land. Attempts have been made to purchase every acre needed by the new comers—very conspicuously in New Zealand. But such attempts never can do justice to the Savage. The savage man from his nature can understand nothing of the real value of the article to be sold. The price must be settled by the purchaser, and he on the other side has no means of ascertaining who in truth has the right to sell, and cannot know to whom the purchase money should be paid. But he does know that he must have the land. He feels that in spreading himself over the earth he is carrying out God's purpose, and has no idea of giving way before this difficulty. He tries to harden his heart against the Savage, and gradually does so in spite of his own conscience. The man is a nuisance and must be made to go.[4]

Put simply, the settlers came to South Africa as robbers and enslavers and they stayed as colonizers. The country belongs to the African people, both by hereditary right and through life-and-death labors extracted from them to build everything that the settlers claim as their own. That the current apartheid system has its origins in the politics of land seizure based on the frontier policy of the settlers from the seventeenth century is not in doubt. The location system, later to be called native reserves, was devised by Sir Theophilus Shepstone as the best way of governing an African population outnumbering the whites by more than ten times.

I have asked the question, why Africans did not experience the fate of other indigenous peoples in settler coloniese? The answer lies first in the wars of resistance that Africans waged in defense of their sovereignty and second in the logic of the capitalist mode of production that developed in South Africa, especially in its relationship with metropolitan Britain. Like European settlers in North America, the white settlers in South Africa fought hard to subjugate the indigenous peoples. But while the whites in North American succeeded in exterminating the better part of the Native American population, the white settlers in South Africa failed. The black people of South Africa—the Xhosa, Zulu, and Sotho Kingdoms—defended themselves with the most heroic and stubborn resistance and received the grudging admiration of Lord Bryce, the British minister who visited South Africa in the late nineteenth century. According to Bryce,

The other set of race troubles, those between white settlers and the aborigines of the land, have been graver in South Africa than any which European governments have had to face in any other new country. The Red man of North America, splendidly as they fought, never seriously checked the advance of the whites. The revolts of the aborigines in Peru and Central America were easily suppressed. The once warlike Maoris of New Zealand have, under the better methods of the last twenty-five years, become quiet and tolerably contented. Even the French in Algeria had not so long a strife to maintain with the Moorish and Kabyle tribes as the Dutch and the English had with the natives of the Cape. The Southcoast kaffirs far outnumbered the whites, were of courage, had a very rough and thickly wooded country to defend. . . . The melancholy chapter of native wars seems now all but closed. . . . These wars, however, did much to retard the progress of South Africa and to give it a bad name. They deterred many an English farmer from emigrating there in the years between 1810–1870. They annoyed and puzzled the home government and made it think of the colony as a worthless possession, whence little profit or credit was to be shown in return for the unending military expenditure.[5]

It took almost two hundred years of unrelenting warfare before the African was defeated; and then only because the best British troops were eventually brought to South Africa with weapons and organization far more advanced than that of the pre-capitalist African society. The African people were unprepared for the brutal effectiveness of the scorched-earch strategy used by the British invaders.

The wars of resistance waged by African kingdoms in the nineteenth century explain why the Europeans in South Africa have remained a minority. In the middle of the nineteenth century, in order to develop the sugar cane plantations in Natal where 4,000 British settlers had been brought in the 1840s, the British brought Indian indentured laborers. These indentured laborers have been described in a book by Hugh Tinker, *The New System of Slavery.*[6] In the United States we know there is a link between the destruction of the North American Indian communities and the introduction of the African slaves. Suppose the African had succumbed, would the East Indian be occupying the position occupied by the Afro-Americans in the USA? I do not want to belabor the point, but I think it is important in any analysis of the political economy of South Africa.

SYNTHETIC CHARACTERIZATION OF SOUTH AFRICA

The characterization of the system of white domination and exploitation in South Africa remains elusive. For liberal writers explanations range from the crude notions of social and cultural pluralisms as primary determinants,[3] to the descriptions of South Africa as a dual society embodying the First World economy and the Third World economy. Earlier liberals were preoccupied with the nature of race prejudice and methods of dealing with it. The neo-Marxist explanations range from the notions of conquest as a determinant, to the simplistic and mechanical application of Poulantzas' class analysis about intracapitalist rivalries, to the relative autonomy of the state, to a modification of the thesis of internal colonialism.

I start with a characterization of South Africa as a settler capitalist social formation, which is the product of the imperialist extension of advanced capitalism. As a dominion, South Africa was originally developed with British capital to fulfill the colonial role of an agrarian auxiliary and source of raw materials for British industrial capitalism. From the standpoint of what I have said in the previous section, white settlers and capitalist development welded South Africa and turned it into a link of the common chain of imperialism. From 1910 to 1961, when South Africa was expelled from the Commonwealth, it enjoyed a special relationship with Britain and other white dominions. R. Palme Dutt[8] described the place of "white" dominions in the British Empire as follows:

> These "White" Dominions, while member states of the Empire, are in effect independent sovereign states or secondary imperialist powers, closely associated with British imperialism, and with British finance-capital interests strongly entrenched in them, but increasingly subject to the counter-pull of American imperialism. Their peoples have in general strong ties of kinship (with the exception of the French-Canadians in Canada and the Afrikaners of Dutch descent in South Africa, as well as, of course, the African and other non-European majority in South Africa), language and tradition with the British people. Their bourgeoisie may be regarded as offshoots of the British bourgeoisie, representing "colonial" settlements in the old Roman sense rather than in the modern sense of subjection and government of alien nations; that is to say, their conquest of the countries they occupy was followed (with the exception of South Africa) by the more or less complete extermination of the original populations, thus turning

their sparsely occupied territories into white settlement territories, within general stringent regulations to limit colored immigration, as in the "White Australia" policy.[9]

Thus, regardless of anything else, the Africans and the European settlers were sharply counterpoised to each other by virtue of their contradictory expectations. The wars fought between Africans and White settlers in the nineteenth century demonstrated how ruthless and irreconcilable was the conflict between the opposing social forces. Dutt[10] refers to the complexity of the situation in the "white" dominions in the sphere of social life, for example, the question of the relations between descendants of the Dutch settlers and English in the case of South Africa and the French and English in Canada; and superimposed on these intra-white conflicts was the fundamental conflict between whites as settlers and blacks as the victims of conquest, dispossession, and exploitation. Within the total set of relations, the problem to British imperialism was to assign to black and white labor different tasks in the productive process reflecting their assumed "inequality" in the scale of evolution!

The problem between black and white in South Africa is posed theoretically as essentially a national one. That is to say, it is a problem of the imposition of alien rule through conquest and the deployment of conquered peoples into various categories of labor power in the settler economy. If we study the actual thrust of South Africa's development from 1875 to 1985, it is possible to determine the underlying principles which shaped the South African society, the organizing principles of the dynamics of its social structures.

The inner logic of South Africa's development was determined not only by the fact that it was first and foremost a settler society but also by the fact that it is a capitalist political economy. The settler population itself was a product of capitalist development in England and elsewhere. In Holland the collapse of feudalism had created displaced and superfluous layers among the peasantry of the seventeenth century. In England the rise of industrial capitalism had displaced many petit-bourgeois farmers in the early part of the nineteenth century. In fact, the 1820 and 1840 settlers were made up mostly of these displaced farmers. The discovery of diamonds (1866) and gold (1884) opened an avenue of escape for certain layers of the British proletariat who were experiencing hard times due to the Depression of the 1870s.

The growing contradictions of capitalism that produced the massive unemployment and growing social discontent in the 1840s in Britain expressed itself in an intensified search for a new homeland for the redundant sectors of the population. For Cecil Rhodes (the founder of the DeBeer's financial empire based on South Africa's diamonds and gold), the colonies provided the British with a safety valve. Speaking to Stead, a journalist friend, Rhodes expressed his fears about the future of England and why he was also a social imperialist:

> I was in the East End of London yesterday and attended a meeting of the unemployed. I listened to the wild speeches, which were just a cry for "bread," "bread," "bread," and on my way home I pondered over the scene and I became more than ever convinced of the importance of imperialism . . . My cherished idea is a solution for the social problem, i.e., in order to save the 40 million inhabitants of the United Kingdom from a bloody civil war, we colonial statesmen must acquire new lands to settle the surplus population, to provide new markets for the goods produced by them in the factories and mines. The Empire, as I have always said, is a bread and butter question. If you want to avoid civil war, you must become imperialists.[11]

In the specific case of British capitalism, the colonies played an exceptional role in relieving internal contradictions. In the age of imperialism the importance of the colonies increased even more, as developments in South Africa illustrate so well.

For example, with the Anglo–Boer War fresh in his mind, J. Hobson, a British economist, described the connections between imperialism and the interest of the "financiers" whose growing profits from contracts, supplies, etc., depended on the empire: "While the directors of this definitely parasitic policy are capitalist," he writes "the same motives appeal to special classes of workers. In many towns the most important traders are dependent upon government employment or contracts; the imperialism of the metal and ship building centers is attributable in no small degree to this fact."[12]

It was at the high noon of imperialism that the then-current vogue of social Darwinism with its doctrine of the struggle for existence and survival of the fittest developed, providing persuasive rationalization for settler colonialism and other expansionist forces.[13] It justified the seizure and exploitation of the lands and people who were considered inferior to Europeans. While politicians like Ernest Chamberlain sang the virtues of economic imperialism, social scientists like Benjamin Kidd and Karl Pearson sang the virtues of social imperialism according to which the struggle of different "races," for instance, was seen as a basic principle of history. Kidd and Pearson asserted that England's first concern—if she meant to maintain her world position—was the welfare of her own people at the expense, if need be, of other "inferior" peoples.[14]

Mr. Cecil Rhodes has been described as the most powerful agent of British imperialism in the late nineteenth century and the bearer of its spirit. Expressing the true sentiment of the time, he wrote:

> I contend that we are the first race in the world, and that the more of the world we inhabit the better it is for the human race. I contend that every acre added to our territory means the birth of the English race who otherwise would not be brought into existence. If there be a God, I think that what he would like me to do is paint as much of the map of Africa British red as possible. . . .[15]

This foray into racist ideas is very important. Feelings of racial superiority infected almost all whites no matter what their class origin. As Huttenback puts it,

> Within the spectrum of Anglo-Saxon prejudice, it was clearly better to be English than Irish, but even more important to be white rather than black. Irishmen and other non-British Europeans might be the objects of opprobrium, but there were at least not as strange and different as the peoples of Africa and Asia.[16]

Huttenback goes on to point out that

> Observers and critics of the British Empire have often been willing to turn a blind eye toward the generally illiberal policies of South Africa because in their view the racial equation there was unique. The fact that the rest of the Empire of Settlement acted similarly has been largely ignored. These colonies, throughout much of the nineteenth century, became the destination of non-Europeans from "friendly" states such as China and Japan and from another part of the British Empire—India. As in South Africa, a strong resentment developed against these new arrivals, based principally on the racial precepts of Anglo-Saxonism but in part also on the workingman's fear of losing his job to "cheap" labor from Africa and Asia.[17]

Two points need emphasis: first, Huttenback makes it possible for us to understand why the Boers in the Treaty of Vereeniging, even though they had been conquered, were given "equality" with the

English settlers; second, it is not surprising that there emerged among white settlers in South Africa, Australia, New Zealand, and Canada a determination (which is still there today) that these areas must be a "white man's country." The "responsible government" given to Canada in 1848 and in the ensuing years to all the parts of the Empire of white settlement was an acknowledgment of the special role white settlers were expected to play in the context of British imperialism.

> All the British colonies of settlement—Canada, Australia, New Zealand and South Africa—were from the first deeply committed to the dream of becoming outposts of the "British race." The only settler to be encouraged to sail to the new lands were British-born denizens of the home islands who shared the ethnic roots and world view of the colonies' white populations. Cruel reality and the laws of economic necessity have, however, a way of eroding and diluting even the most firmly held beliefs, and as labor became an ever more compelling need in the vast and sparsely settled imperial lands, entrepreneurs came to the realization that the reservoir of manpower in Britain willing to settle overseas was not great enough to fulfill the demands. Besides, the ease of acquiring land, as Edward Gibbon Wakefield so clearly saw, invited the dispersal of what white population there was and prevented the establishment of a labor pool upon which employers could draw. And in the only colony with a large native population, Natal, the tribes resident in the territory were unwilling to provide continuous and reliable labor.[18]

The second logic of South Africa's social development is offered by the nature of South Africa's economic development as a capitalist social formation. While it is true that South Africa's fortunes were determined by developments in European politics and economy going back to the seventeenth century, the breadth and depth of this influence changed considerably after the discovery of diamonds and gold. To exploit the diamond and gold, British imperialism delivered to South Africa monopoly capitalism ready-made including the skilled miners. With rifle and bayonet British imperialism also drove the African peasants and Boer farmers from their subsistence environment straight into capitalist exploitation. The evolution of the settler state is closely bound up with the requirements of the political economy of capitalism based on the most gigantic mineral extraction in the world.

Whether South Africa was going to be the "white man's" country in the sense of the United States, Australia, or New Zealand or in the political sense, became a serious issue in the last quarter of the nineteenth century. A great debate began in England regarding the future of the African in the South African colonies. The various options of what to do with the Africans are summed up by Trollope (in the work already referred to) as follows:

> What is our duty to the Kafir or Zulu? There are so many views of our duty! One believes that we have done the important thing if we teach him to sing hymns. Another would give him back say a tenth of the land that has been taken away from him, and then leave him. A third, the most confident of them all, thinks that everything hangs on "a rod of iron," between which and slavery the distance is very narrow. The rod of iron generally means compelled work, the amount of wages to be settled by the judgment of the master. A fourth would give him franchise and let him vote for a Member of Parliament which of course includes the privilege of becoming a Member of Parliament, and of becoming Prime Minister if he can get enough of his own class to back him. [19]

Before the discovery of diamonds in 1867, South Africa "was an impoverished bundle of colonies and Boer republics perched on a savage continent. Cape Town may have been called the Mother City, but the town that gave birth to the modern state of South Africans was Kimberly," Jessup noted. [20] It was the genius of Trollope to foresee this. Indeed, the discovery of diamonds in Kimberley gave new support to those who favored the 'iron-rod' solution to the "Native Question." By 1875, the Kimberley mines were already employing 3,500 African miners. Trollope, who visited Kimberley in 1877, saw these black miners hard at work and became hypnotized by the prospect of the future use of African labor in the mines and other industries that mining generally spawned. Waxing eloquent about the virtues of work as a civilizing agent Trollope wrote:

> Who can doubt but that work is the great civilizer of the world— work and the growing desire for those good things which work only will bring? If there be one who does he should come here to see now those dusky troops of laborers, who ten years since were living in the wildest state of unalloyed savagery, whose only occupation was the slaughter of each other in tribal wars, each of whom was the slave of his Chief, who were subject to the dominion of most brutalizing and cruel superstitions, have

already put themselves on the path toward civilization. They are
thieves no doubt—that is they steal diamonds though not often
other things. They are not Christians. They do not yet care much
about breeches. They do not go to school. But they are orderly.
They come to work at six in the morning and go away at six in the
evening. They have an hour in the middle of the day, and know
that they have to work during the other hours. They take their
meals regularly and, what is the best of all, they are learning to
spend their money instead of carrying it back to their Chiefs.[21]

In a paragraph before this, after criticizing the slowness of "philan-
thropy and religion in civilizing the savages," Trollope makes the
point that

The seeker after diamonds is determined to have them [Africans]
because the making of his fortune depends upon them; and the
Kafir himself is determined to come to Kimberly because he has
learned the loveliness of 10s. a week paid regularly into his hand
every Saturday Night.[22]

Trollope prophesied further employment of Africans in other mining
ventures in the future

We have fair reason to believe that other similar industries will
arise. There are already copper mines at work in Namaqualand,
on the western coast of South Africa, in which the Natives are
employed, and lead mines in the Transvaal. There are gold fields
in the Transvaal at which little is now being done, because the
difficulties of working them are at present overwhelming. But as
years roll quickly on these, too, will become hives of coloured
labour, and in this way Kimberleys will arise in various parts of
the continent.[23]

It could be argued that Trollope was expressing his own racist
sentiment, in no way representative of British imperialism. Placed in
the context of all the events which were taking place and which would
make South Africa a 'white man's country', Trollope expressed the
thinking of the times.[24]

Alexander Wilmot, a Cape Town politician and a fellow of the Royal
Geographical Society, in 1895, not only stressed racial solidarity,
migration, and conquest in justifying White political supremacy, but
the importance of White exploitation of "colored" labor.

The existence of the coloured race is an immense benefit, as, by means of them, cheap labour is obtainable, and large agricultural supplies can be constantly procured; but Southern Africa, although its population chiefly comprises the descendants of stalwart nomadic races who have migrated from a northern part of the continent, is eminently a white man's country, where homes can be found for millions of the overflowing population of Europe.[25]

I have already referred to Cecil Rhodes' social imperialist view. Let me now briefly refer to his political views toward the African population. For instance, in moving the second reading of the Glen Grey Bill, Cecil Rhodes, Prime Minister and also Minister of Native Affairs in the government of the Cape colony, favored the sentiment of those who preferred the "rod of iron." Arguing against the policy of extermination he said:

If you are one who really likes the natives you must make them worthy of the country they live in, or else they are certain, by an inexorable law, to lose their country, you will certainly not make them worthy if you allow them to sit in idleness and if you do not train them in the arts of civilization.[26]

In forthright and unequivocal terms, Rhodes set forth the principles that would guide black/white political relations to the present.

I will lay down my policy on the Native question . . . either you will receive them on an equal footing as citizens or call them a subject race. . . . I have made up my mind that there must be class (race) legislation. . . . The Native is to be treated as a child and denied the franchise. We must adopt the system of despotism. . . . These are my policies and these are the politics of South Africa.[27]

If we ask the question: through what sorts of mechanisms did racism become articulated in the very organization of South Africa's white society; we cannot ignore the fact that racism, economic exploitation, and social degradation are so closely intertwined that it does not make sense to treat them as independent variables.

In short, the genocidal wars of the nineteenth century stopped at the point where their logic might have been detrimental to the labor needs of imperialist. According to Cairns:

> The Africans, unlike the American Indian or the Australian aborigines, were expected to play a permanent role in future economic development. Consequently, theories justifying their extermination lacked utility, and accordingly were not employed. In essence, the use of evolutionary theories stopped at the point where their employment might have been detrimental to European interests.[28]

The position the African occupies in South Africa today reveals a tension between the logic of settler colonialism; extermination and, the need for his labor power ("protection"?). The treatment of Africans as a subject race became a policy of the settler state not because of racial prejudice as some would have us believe but, rather, because it would be economically profitable to the likes of Rhodes, while also safeguarding the interest of the expatriate white settlers.

It was Adam Smith who argued that a colonial system embodies in exaggerated form the virtues and vices of the metropolitan power. The English, in their settler colony of South Africa, reproduced the structural defects of the metropolitan class structure. Lord Milner, high commissioner for South Africa and governor of the Cape and Transvaal colonies (1897–1905), was very clear about the type of society he wanted in South Africa. He argued in favor of a social and political order in which the interest of the White settlers would be paramount.

> We do not want a white proletariat in this country. The position of the whites among the vastly more numerous black population requires that even their lowest ranks should be able to maintain a standard of living far above that of the poorest section of the population of a purely white country. . . . However you look at the matter, you always come back to the same root principle— the urgency of that development which alone can make this a white man's country in the only sense in which South Africa can become one, and that is, not a country full of poor whites, but one in which a largely increased white population can live in decency and comfort. That development requires capital, but it also requires a large amount of rough labour. And that labour cannot to any extent, be white, if only because, pending development and the subsequent reduction in the cost of living, white labour is much too dear.[29]

Given their views, it is not surprising that Milner and those who worked with him left South Africa a colonial structure of exploitation unique in history. In his single-minded pursuit of imperialist interest, Milner threw all integrity and morality to the wind and did not hesitate to use the most perverse logic. On his return to England he became a peer and a member of the Coefficient Club—rewarded for an imperial job well done.[30]

The policy of British imperialism was reckless and irresponsible, but not by chance and not because of subjective mistakes of one leader or another. The nature of the views of Rhodes, Milner, and the rest historically reflected the assumptions of imperialism. Make no mistake about it, African subordination was carefully planned. Marxists understand that black inequality was enshrined in the Union Constitution because of the enormous benefits that the bourgeoisie derive from it. And the African people, placed under the heel of imperial capital, would pay tribute in unbelievable torment and suffering.

The result of Milner's policies in South Africa is well known. The resulting subordination of blacks founded and retained by British imperialism was accepted by white labor, and became a basis of a system of capitalism which made the attainment of democracy impossible. The price of the arrangement was to make the white population as a whole the social base for the indirect exploitation of South Africa's mineral and other resources by imperialism. The racial character of capitalist development in South Africa, premised on a system of exploitation designed to provide unlimited supplies of cheap black labor to all white employers, created conditions of national oppression. The differential wage scales imposed for different grades of labor made the formation of a common labor organization for white and black almost impossible.

The phenomenon whereby the British ruling class bought off and politically corrupted some sections of the working class is well known and was commented upon several times in the nineteenth century. Lenin coined the concept of the "aristocracy of labor" from practices of the British ruling classes and from similar practices in the "white"parts of the British Empire. The "aristocracy of labor" is a privileged stratum of the working class.

> It arises when economic circumstances of capitalism make it possible to grant significant concessions to its proletariat, within which certain strata of workers manage, by means of their special scarcity, skill, strategic position, organizational strength, etc. to establish notably better conditions for themselves than the rest.[31]

Further, Lenin's theory of imperialism argues that the "handful of the richest, privileged nations" turned into "parasites on the body of the rest of mankind," that is, into collective exploiters, and suggest a division of the world into "exploiting" and "proletarian" nations. Lenin also reminds us that the original Roman proletariat was a collectively parasitic class and "lived at the expense of society."[32]

What happened in South Africa was not something new. Already in 1858 Engels sarcastically described the tamed British workers as follows:

> The English proletariat is actually becoming more bourgeois, so that this most bourgeois of all nations is apparently aiming ultimately at the possession of a bourgeois artistocracy and a bourgeois proletariat alongside the bourgeoisie. For a nation which exploits the whole world, this is to a certain extent justified.[33]

With minor modificatons, the above characterization of the labor aristocracy in England described the settler social and class system.[34] Stein and Stein,[35] referring to the colonial heritage in Latin America, may well describe the class structure of South Africa as it emerged from conquest and what sociologists call social engineering.

> The social heritage of settler colonialism [in South Africa] was not merely a rigid structure of an elite of wealth, status and power at the apex, and at the bottom a pyramid, a mass of poverty-stricken, marginal, powerless, and subordinate people. Such societies have flourished everywhere. The tragedy of the colonial heritage was a social structure further stratified by color and physiognomy—by what anthropologists call phenotype: an elite of whites and a mass of people of color—coloreds (mixed blood), Indians, and Africans—in that ascending order. The British imperial bourgeoisie, like their North American counterparts had come to understand that a society may perpetuate social inequalities and injustices far more effectively when the maldistribution of income is buttressed by phenotype.

In sum then, practices and habits of thought nurtured over centuries and handed down from one generation of exploiters to another are not easily forgotten. The social relations by which all Africans are subordinated to whites are deeply implicated with class and racial structures. They are also shot through with contradictions. Although intra-class differences have developed within each of the three officially defined "races," the defining feature of South Africa is white rule which can also be defined as racially-structured capitalism. As Legassick[36] put it:

> The structures of South Africa sustain a situation in which it is whites (although not all whites) who are the accumulators of capital, the wealthy, and the powerful, while the majority of blacks (though not all blacks) are the unemployed, the ultra-exploited, the poor and the powerless.

The South African state reflected the interest of a relatively independent, stratified white society, based on exploitation of the black population with a legitimating ideology of white superiority. Interclass white politics would redress, at least for the white working class, the inequality generated by "free-market" capitalism without endangering the interests of imperialism.

The Act of Union, which handed political power to white settlers, enabled them after 1910 to establish a pattern of "race" relations which insured that in every respect the African served white interests. As Simons and Simons[37] put it:

> Parliamentary government in a racially stratified society made white interests paramount. If universal suffrage produces a welfare state under capitalism, white suffrage gives rise under colonialism to a colour-bar state. A political party that appeals to white voters alone invariably make their claims the touchstone of policy, plays on their collective fears of black power, excites and reinforces their racial antagonisms, and consolidates them into a hegemonic bloc in opposition to the voteless majority.

The Jim Crow system in the US offers a useful analogy to the system of segregation and apartheid in South Africa. It was imposed by denying and disenfranchising black voters through segregation and fraud and denial of their citizenship rights. According to Barnes,

> The Jim Crow system at its fullest development was the attempt in the states of the old Confederacy to institutionalize, codify in law, and make permanent the expropriation and oppression of Black people—the freed slaves and their descendants—by separating them from all economic, social, and political activity engaged in by white people. Its purpose was to make it as

difficult as possible for Blacks to become free farmers, and to
make it impossible for them to ever compete on an equal basis
with white workers in selling their labor power to the capitalists.[38]

It should be clear from the preceding discussion that no analysis of
the historical and contemporary situation of Africans in South Africa
would be adequate which failed to recognize the important role of
British imperialism then and now in creating the conditions for black
subordination, both in the overall division of labor and the racist
ideological forms which have accompanied that position.

The indulgence that the various British administrations give the
erstwhile settler state of South Africa is not surprising. According to
Romero Daniels,

> Britain has direct constitutional responsibility in creating the
> fascist state in SA. Its occupation of the Cape Colony in 1806,
> ensured that the Africans were brutally exploited and dispossessed
> of their land through military conquest. The Africans were
> disenfranchised and deliberately excluded from the profit and
> wealth which they themselves helped to create. As if it was not
> enough, Britain blessed "Voortrekers" to establish their own evil
> Boer republics, by the 1852 Sand River Convention, and the
> 1854 Bloemfontein Convention. The main term of agreement in
> both conventions, was that both the Boer entities and British
> Cape Colony were to wage a war of disarmament against the
> Africans and maintenance of the Masters and Servants Act.[39]

In what ways are the concrete conditions of exploitation of black
labor, as a fraction of the South African working class, essentially
different from those of white labor? How significant are those
differences, in both qualitative and quantitative terms? And how were
these differences connected with the expanded reproduction and
development of racial capitalism? The study of the South African
mining industry, especially gold mining, is extremely important and
provides answers to these questions.

THE SOCIAL LEGACY OF DIAMONDS AND GOLD

Let me discuss the logic of South Africa's most important industry—
diamond and gold mining. As Barrington Moore, Jr.[40] observed in
1967, certain forces of capitalist transformations may succeed eco-

nomically in the sense of yielding good profits, but are for fairly obvious reasons unfavorable to the growth of the free institutions of the old capitalist societies. This happens, he says, when the ruling classes maintain intact the preexisting peasant society, introducing only enough change in the rural society to ensure that the peasants generate a sufficient surplus which can be appropriated and marketed along the lines of the basic plantation "model" of mercantile capitalism. Moore further points out that "Straightforward slavery in modern times is likely to be the creation of a class of colonizing intruders into tropical areas."[41]

The distinction between "labor-repressive" versus "market" labor recruitment is at the heart of the explanation of different patterns and outcomes of modernization. "Reactionary capitalist" modernization is possible, according to Moore, if a country is invaded by mature capital, greedy to make super-profits.[42] In other words, territorial expansion of capital not only opened up new opportunities for investment, the 'home' state was often called in by investors to create a political and judicial environment suitable for their activities.

Can an understanding of plantation economics be useful in studying mining economies? In South Africa there is a symbiosis which links gold and diamond mining to African servitude. Many writers have produced convincing arguments that diamond and gold mining industries, like plantation systems, provided imperatives to reduce black workers to servile conditions.

According to Johnstone,

> Gold was the key to South Africa's 'great transformation' into an advanced industrial economy and a modern system of racial domination. And the story of gold encapsulates and symbolizes much of the larger story of South Africa. It is what I have referred to . . . as the "play within a play," which as in *Hamlet* starkly reveals certain underlying themes, themes, which here, unlike in Hamlet, are about capital, labour, exploitation, and what Engels, in his initial investigation of the first "great transformation" called "social murder."[43]

The secret of the power of gold lies in the fact that for centuries it symbolized wealth and the most absolute, tangible and universal form of money. From the 1890s until World War II and, to a lesser extent, even today gold mining has been the fulcrum, the privileged expression of South Africa's political economy. It is no accident that the story of the Rand (the gold mining industry of the Witwatersrand) has figured prominently in the class analysis of racial domination. Marx summed up the role of a key industry like gold as follows:

> There is in every social formation a particular branch of production which determines the position and importance of all others, and the relations of all other branches as well. It is as though light of a particular hue were cast upon everything, tinging all other colors and modifying their specific features; or as if either determined the specific gravity of everything found in it.[44]

The study of the developing social relations in the gold mining industry provides clues, not only to an understanding of the South African society and its class and national conflicts, but its links through gold with the world imperialist system:

> The Anglo–American Corporation of South Africa—the world's biggest mining finance empire—sprawls across Africa from Cape Town in the south to the shores of Lake Victoria in the northwest. Its mining activities cover America, the frozen wastes of Canada and the arid land of Australia. Its sinew of development, Anglo–American money, is finely woven into the business texture of England and intertwined with the major financial centers of Europe.[45]

The configuration of South Africa's capitalism around gold mining, the one industry most infiltrated by foreign capital in search of usurious returns, had serious implications. Gold mining in particular established an organic ascendency over the other sectors of the economy becoming, as it were, the "heart" of South Africa's political economy, thanks to its organic link with outside capital. Until recently the role of external finance capital enjoyed relative autonomy from the domestic polity. In 1910 when South Africa became "independent," the "heart" of its capitalism stood independent from the very "body" it controlled so easily, resting upon its great institutional and international strength and its world network of world interests.[46]

From the gold mining industry, civil society derived its poisonous nourishment and its distinctive character. Through the poisonous nourishment provided by gold profits and dividends the economy grew to be the deformed monster that it is today. Pyrah describes the impact of the discovery of gold in South Africa:

> The discovery of diamonds and more particularly gold on the

Rand in 1886, wrought an economic revolution which precipitated a new crisis in, and gave a new complexion to, almost every
feature of South African life. As the mining community increased,
an industrial economy came to be founded on permanent lines in
the heart of the Boer country. It brought into salient relief the
deep opposition of the Old Africa and the new, of the farms and
the mines, of the Afrikaners and the British. Two types of
civilization, conforming largely to the racial division, came face
to face. In such a situation the reverberations of clashing
interests, attended with impatients or irritation, might easily
cause a collision; and after the British occupation of Southern
Rhodesia there no longer remained an outlet, a new unsettled
hinterland, whither the Boer people could trek in order to
preserve themselves and their institutions inviolate from the
march of modern industrialism.[47]

To understand the importance of South Africa's gold finds, we need
to remind ourselves that South Africa was and is the gold-based
economy of the world. As R.W. Johnson puts it:

Gold is the overwhelmingly visible, nay tangible, fact of South
African life. Her greatest city, Johannesburg, is, in every sense,
built on it. Her largest company, Anglo–American, owes its
position to its ownership of two-fifths of the mines; the mining
operations are vast and employ some 700,000 people. Of the
economically active workforce in 1960 one in every seven men
and one in every twelve women (of all races) worked in mining.
It is, above all, the dominant fact of life for urban African men. In
1960, of all such men who had jobs, more than one in every three
worked in the mining sector.[48]

Three-quarters of the gold produced in the entire history of gold
mining has been produced since the 1890's: that is precisely in the
epoch when the South African gold mines were discovered and began
to be exploited. Today South Africa produces almost seventy-four
percent of the world capitalist supply of gold. Until the 1940s, gold was
the cornerstone of foreign exchange and primitive capital accumulation
for South Africa itself. The crucial and strategic importance of gold
therefore, points to its other important aspect—it is not only an
industry most penetrated by foreign capital, it is also a privileged
industry in South Africa itself.

What social and political structures were established to make gold mining profitable?

In relation to other sectors of the South Africa economy, the gold mining industry presents unique racist features: (1) it used large quantities of black, cheap labor supervised at strategic points by a small elite of white skilled workers and (2) its entire output is destined for foreign consumption rather than local use. Thus, in the historic conditions that formed South Africa's political economy of racial capitalism in the last decades of the nineteenth century, in her conquest, her classes, her state, in the continuing dependence of her gold industry on imperialist investment, we ought to locate an important dimension perpetuating her structures of racial exploitation and social inequality. For South Africa, the gold industry is capital par excellence; for its expansion and preservation everything was done, including the mobilization of labor from China and the whole of Southern Africa.

In what ways did the gold industry "modify the specific features" of South Africa's political economy? The gold mining industry is notorious not only for the most reckless use of African labor but also for the shameless use of racial exploitation. It is not an exaggeration to say that many of the patterns of racial exploitation currently practiced in other industries can be attributed to the dominant influence of the productive relations first articulated and formulized in the mining industry. The following formulation by Marx with minor modification as indicated, describes the importance of gold in the political economy of South Africa.

> The specific economic form in which surplus labor is pumped out of direct producers [in the mines], determines the relationship of rulers and ruled, as it grows directly out of production itself and, in turn, reacts upon it as a determining element. Upon [the relations in the gold industry] ... is founded the entire formation of the economic community which grows up out of the production relations themselves, thereby simultaneously its specific political form. [49]

He goes on to say:

> It is always the direct relationship of the owners of the conditions of production to the direct producers—a relation always naturally corresponding to a definite stage in the development of the methods of labour and thereby its social productivity—which

reveals the innermost secret, the hidden basis of the entire social structure, and with it the political form of the relation of sovereignty and dependence, in short, the corresponding specific form of the state. This does not prevent the same economic basis—the same from the standpoint of its main conditions—due to innumerable different empirical circumstances, natural environment, racial relations, external historical influences, etc., from showing infinite variations and gradations in appearance, which can be ascertained only by analysis of the empirically given circumstances.[50]

For South Africa as a whole, the most important domestic development after the discovery of diamonds and gold was the elaboration of racial laws to make these two mining ventures profitable. The blighting effects of the mining industry in association with farming in time, profoundly affected all segments of the political economy.

Gold mining, the domain of extreme exploitation, produced violence, plunder, and enslavement of the work force which is unequalled in the history of the primitive accumulation of capital. For instance, Cecil Rhodes and De Beers management introduced a novel system which, according to H.J. Simons and Ray Simons has become a classic system of labor control and theft prevention in the South African mines.

They hit on the idea of confining African miners in closed compounds for four or six months of their contract period. . . . The compound was an enclosure surrounded by a high corrugated iron fence and covered by wire-netting. The men lived, twenty to a room, in huts or iron cabins built against the fence. They went to work along a tunnel, bought food and clothing from the company's stores, and received free medical treatment but no wages during sickness, all within the compounds. Men due for discharge were confined in detention rooms for several days, during which they wore only blankets and fingerless leather gloves padlocked to their wrists, swallowed purgatives, and were examined for stones concealed in cuts, wounds, swellings and orifices.[51]

It was Marx who foretold in a classic way the fate that awaited indigenous workers in mining operations.

The discovery of gold and silver in America, the extirpation, enslavement and entombment in mines of the aboriginal population, the beginning of conquest and the looting of East Indies, the turning of Africa into a warren for commercial hunting of black skin signalized the rosy dawn of the era of capitalist production. These idyllic proceedings are the chief momento of primitive accumulation. This phase of the accumulation process was accomplished not only by domestic exploitation but also by the looting of traditional stores of non-European peoples, and fostering a new system of slavery to exploit their labor.[52]

In South Africa the extraction of diamonds and gold created an insatiable demand for cheap labor and accelerated conquest which turned Southern Africa, south of the twenty-second parallel, into a huge reserve for commercial recruitment of black bodies, thousands of whom have since been entombed in the deep bowels of the South African gold mines. Fortunes were made overnight; the wealth made in South Africa's mining is phenomenal. As Frankel in 1938 observed, "The wealth accruing from the production of diamonds in South Africa has probably been greater than that which has ever been attained from any other commodity in the same time anywhere in the world."[53]

If all the accumulated capital from the profits of gold is added to this, the magnitude of the wealth produced by black labor becomes gigantic indeed.

To Keynes, gold was a "barbarous relic" and indeed it is. Yet it forms the backbone of South Africa's political economy. But if the South African mines were elsewhere they would not be worked. Hance, an American geographer, writes "If the gold reefs (of the Rand) were situated in the United States, they probably would be of interest only to students of geology; they would not be worked."[54]

Why then are the South African mines still being worked? The reason was given over a decade ago by *Newsweek*:

The gold that everyone is talking about comes mostly from South Africa, where this year 400,000 blacks supervised by 36,000 whites mined about 729 metric tons, or about 23 million ounces, worth $4.2 billion. That is more than half of the world's total yearly output. Six powerful financial houses run the apartheid nation's 42 gold mines, and they make a good profit mainly because of the abundance of cheap, black African labor. For every metric ton of gold that is produced, more than 100,000 tons of ore must be brought to the surface—often from depths as great as two miles—milled.[55]

BRITISH IMPERIALISM AND THE GOLD MINING INDUSTRY

The discovery of gold and diamonds revealed the real intentions of British imperialism in South Afria. It initiated the conquest and unification of the country. Thus the period from 1870 until the turn of the century was marked by a wave of aggressive wars launched by Britain and its Cape Colony to dominate the entire subcontinent. Thereafter Britain utilized the territory as a primary area of investment and, indeed, until recently, British and American interests have controlled the bulk of capital investments in the gold mines.

The central fact about the South African economy after the discovery of gold in 1886 would be its domination by British capital— by British imperialism. It was from its domination by British financial interests that the specific characteristics of the South African political economy flowered. After 1910 the white settlers were politically in control, but the British owned the diamond mines, the gold mines, and the railways that transported these minerals. Thus, the country's basic industry, its "heart," was a British appendage. Through control of the gold industry, British imperialism had power without responsibility. British imperialism wanted to exploit South Africa's gold on "easy," predatory terms, thanks to the almost slave-like conditions to which black miners had been reduced by racism.

In South Africa as elsewhere the British took care to permanently tighten this hold over the entire region before giving political control to the Boers. Duncan Innes explains how British supremacy was established. What he says is so important that it deserves quoting at length.

> It is not always appreciated in commentaries on this period of South African history—particularly by those who interpret it in terms of a conflict between modes of production—that the key to understanding why events unfolded as they did lies in recognizing the specific form of the international capitalist relations of *monopoly* capitalism. It is this which explains why the gold mining industry developed on such a large scale in South Africa: why it was possible for gold ore of very low grade, buried deep in the earth's crust under thick layers of hard rock, to be removed and profitably exploited; why it was possible for the resistance of millions of black people to be broken; why it was possible not only to control these people but also to discipline them so that their labour would be sufficiently cheap for the industry to develop on a profitable basis; why it was possible to prevent the advantages secured by highly paid, organized skilled workers

> from permeating through to other sectors of the workforce; how
> it was possible for the labour and other economic needs of the
> mining industry to be secured without destroying other local
> industries, such as agriculture and infrastructure, on which
> mining also depended; and, finally, how it was possible to secure
> all this while at the same time securing sufficient political
> influence in the region to ensure the social and political stability
> on which the future reproduction of the industry was equally
> dependent. These were no mean achievements. They amounted
> to no less than the greatest social revolution ever carried out on
> the African continent. Their effect is still felt today in the daily
> lives of many millions of people.[56]

The most important point to make is that white settler domination
and capitalist development has been built on a legacy of ruthless wars
of subjugation and enslavement of African kingdoms, on indentured
Indian labor, on contract labor from China; and as a legacy, on a system
of migrant labor which relied on impoverished African peasants held
prisoner on reservations as a main source of cheap and profitable
labor. The migrant labor system was reinforced by the pass system and
extended to embrace all the British colonies, the Protectorates, and the
Portuguese colonies.

In the last one hundred years, the lot of Africans in South Africa has
been dictated by the interests of imperial marauders. Their will has
been bludgeoned and coerced under some of the most vicious forms
of human exploitation ever inflicted upon one people by another.
Their material poverty is a vivid memorial of its opposite—the
extraordinary quantity of material wealth which their labors have
produced and which has been stolen from them, particularly in the
gold mines.

THE EVOLUTION OF A THEORY OF THE SOUTH AFRICAN REVOLUTION

The history of South Africa is a history of armed resistance by Africans,
first in defense of the sovereignty of their chiefdoms and kingdoms.
This phase of the struggle lasted for almost two hundred years. Their
assegai, knobkerry, and ox-shield were no match for imperial Britain's
maxim gun. Following their defeat in the last quarter of the nineteenth
century and the incorporation of their men and womenfolk into the
settler economy, the political struggle against settler domination and
class exploitation was joined.

The Black struggle was a struggle against national oppression and
exploitation. I have already referred to Lenin's summation of the world

created by imperialism which he said was divided into oppressed and oppressor nations. Given the integration of South Africa into the world economy, the struggle against national oppression and exploitation became indistinguishable from, and as one with, the struggle against imperialism. Prior to the creation of the Union, various congresses representing ethnic formations emerged: the Coloured People's Organization, the South African Indian Congress, and the Native Congress in the Cape, Transvaal, and Natal, which in 1912 merged to form the Native National Congress, later to be called the African National Congress. Today, the South African liberation, headed by the ANC, is a multiclass alliance embracing these ethnic movements; it draws inspiration from two modern political currents—nationalism and socialism.[57]

The fundamental problem that faced the African National Congress in 1912, two years after the creation of the exclusive white Union of South Africa, was one of developing unity and a national formation among hitherto independent African groups and communities. As independent and divided groups, Africans, Colored, and Indians would stay vulnerable and would not be able to resolve the vital problems that white settler domination imposed for their survival. Africans fragmented by language differences, balkanized into ethnic communities, would not be able to accept the challenge of history. Coloreds and Indians placed as a buffer between Africans and the whites could always be used as scapegoats. How were these groups to be united? The rulers of the recently defeated kingdoms and the educated elite resolved in the first conference of all the peoples of South Africa to lay the basis for national unity.

The African struggle for national and social emancipation developed dialectically from the contradictions inherent in the nature of settler colonialism and capitalist exploitation. Settler colonialism as we have seen creates a three-fold national question. It deprives a whole people or peoples of their birthright of their land. Second, the process of development of conquered peoples is not only frozen, but in fact attempts are made to force them to regress. Not just feudal autarchy but tribal autarchy was systematically imposed on African chiefdoms and kingdoms. That is what the so-called "self-development" schemes of the Bantustans are all about. Third, there is the gross exploitation of Africans by local and imperial capital. The development of monopoly capital as the dominant form of capital in the South African gold mines imposed usurious conditions on black workers. Here is an industry where black workers are reduced into labor units in a manner so profound it is perhaps inconceivable. The pass system, the mining compound, and the migrant labor system typify this gross injustice and exploitation. In other words, South Africa is a mirror, an intense magnification of social oppression and degradation of capitalism under colonial conditions.

Only by taking into account the totality of African experience under white settler colonialism and capitalist exploitation can one begin to understand the theory of the South African revolution and the nature of the African National Congress that has spearheaded African resistance in the past seventy-five years. In 1910, Africans were not only politically powerless, they were also disarmed and excluded from military or police training. The era since 1910 had left the Africans in very much the state of the nineteenth-century English agricultural laborer described by Thorold Rogers:

> . . . scattered and incapable of combined action with his fellows, bowed down by centuries of oppression, hard usage and hard words, with every social force against him, the league with the farmers and the clergymen in league with both, the latter constantly preaching resignation, the two former constantly enforcing it, he has lived through evil times.[58]

The South African National liberation movement, headed by the ANC, has after seventy-five years, emerged as the only champion of true democracy and national reconciliation. The Freedom Charter adopted by the Congress Alliance in 1955 not only declares that South Africa belongs to all who live in it, but also that the wealth of the country belongs to the producers of that wealth. The South African liberation movement, forged in the crucible of the barbarities of white racism and the mean spirit of capitalism, and tempered in the heat of bitter national and class struggles, is demonstrating with each passing day its capacity to undertake the profound historical task of the Freedom Charter which will lead South Africa to genuine freedom.[59]

The most important thesis of the theory of the South African revolution lays bare the relationship between national oppression and capitalist exploitation. The *Strategy and Tactics* of the ANC, adopted in Morogoro in 1969, elaborates further the Freedom Charter, arguing emphatically that the national and class dimensions in South Africa are inseparable, neither can be stressed at the expense of the other; they must be resolved simultaneously.

CONCLUSIONS

In looking at South Africa today, there is no doubt that white minority rule is facing its deepest crisis. It is a picture of the masses of black people no longer willing to accept the daily life of apartheid and all that this concept means. The struggle is breaking out in new and broader dimensions, drawing people from all sections of the communities of South Africa, including some whites, into the struggle. The struggle has heightened fears about the potential not only for civil war but about the future of capitalism in South Africa. The momentous nature of the developing revolution is that it confronts imperialism with the most difficult choices. South Africa is a pillar not only of imperialist interest in southern Africa; in the geopolitics of the East-West confrontation, it has been assigned a crucial place.

The implications of the South African struggle for the imperialist world were recently summed up as follows by *The Nation Magazine* and deserve quoting at some length.

South Africa lives in the mind of America as a symbol, a warning and a hope: in the imagery of the familiar folk lyric, a hammer, a bell and a song. The symbol is of both an ending and a beginning. The hammer of revolution set to strike at some still unforeseeable hour represents not only the last act of the decolonization of the continent, but the genesis of a new struggle to shape African history.

The warning sounds for the global system of political alliances and economic interests headquartered in Washington. Political and financial powers in the United States think of South Africa as an outpost of the Western empire, a cornerstone of that empire's strategy and a trustee of its "civilization." White South African leaders may harbor resentments, but they know they cannot survive outside the orbit, that they must live in uneasy dependence on the self-interest, if not the kindness, of strangers in another land.

The hope is that a victory against apartheid in South Africa can be shared by others similarly oppressed. There is a worldwide apartheid that expresses on a grand though less obvious scale the prejudices, the priorities and the restrictions of the diabolitical model developed in Pretoria. A "white" minority controls the wealth, monopolizes the weapons and determines the crucial policies for a dark majority of the earth. (As in South Africa, other ethnic groups, such as the Japanese, may attain honorary membership in the master race if they acquire enough strength.) The rich and powerful developed and now defend a network of theoretically independent homeland-nations for the poor and powerless, and within that network, immigration and the division of labor is strictly regulated. The concepts of "influx control" and "illegal immigrants" apply equally to Soweto and San Antonio. What benefits the rulers bestow on their benighted subjects come from the perception of their self-interest rather than from any sense of collective justice or equity.[60]

The United States and its allies seem to be at a loss as to what to do about the deteriorating situation in South Africa. They have called for stability and reform, lest the country "fall" to forces led by the African National Congress, which given its Freedom Charter, would disrupt profits, not only nationally but regionally as well. Their nightmare is a black revolution sweeping to a successful conclusion across South Africa and spreading its influence to its next logical places: the racist metropolises of England, France, and the ghettoes of the United States.

Apartheid in South Africa reveals, not so much the excesses of global inequalities and economic injustices, but its naked brutality. The basis of the London-Washington-Tel Aviv/Pretoria axis is not simply economic in the narrow sense (for example, the fact that South Africa supplies the capitalist West with gold and other strategic minerals), but a question of class survival in the larger sense. This motivates, above all, the imperialist drive to halt the gains of African independence and reverse the process which seems to lead inexorably toward an African socialist revolution. In the proxy-war to save white minority rule and capitalism in southern Africa, Angola has become an important battle ground for the future of the African revolution.

Much has already been said and written about the policy of "constructive engagement." No doubt, the assumption of power by the Reagan Administration, willing to defy world public opinion in its support of racist South Africa, soon after the collapse of Portuguese colonialism and the independence of Zimbabwe, was a welcome development in Pretoria. The policy of "constructive engagement" provided the Botha regime with the moral support it so desperately needed to save itself from inevitable doom.

Strictly speaking, there is nothing new about the concept of "constructive engagement." Since the early 1960s, successive American administrations have made their own contribution to the consolidation of relations with the racist regime and to building it into a bastion of anticommunism in Africa. South Africa is today a nuclear power, thanks to the American support; the South African arms industry was built with technology and patents sold by the Western countries, who defied the UN embargoes. But, as distinct from its predecessors, the Reagan Administration decided to dispense with hypocrisy. It declared from the outset that American relations with South Africa would be built on the basis of its global confrontation with the USSR.

This meant rapprochement with Pretoria, scuttling the Namibian independence until a formula was found that would reintegrate Angola into the South African sphere of influence. Only then would Namibia be given a settlement advantageous to the United States and South Africa. In the meantime, South Africa would be encouraged to make cosmetic reforms that would help to split and neutralize the African National Congress. Eventually it was hoped that under U.S. tutelage southern Africa would again revert back to the previous state of affairs—become a "belt" of pro-Western regimes politically and economically dependent on South Africa—the regional settler-type gendarme for Western imperialism.

The most explicit formulation of this policy was supplied by an instruction issued for the internal use of the Radio Free Europe Station, excerpts of which were printed in the *Washington Post*: "However wicked apartheid may be," it said, "South Africa, unlike the USSR, does not constitute a menace to the Free World, and its system does not require aggression against foreign countries to assure survival. Pretoria has intervened in neighboring states to remove threats to its own borders, but it has not tried to export apartheid." The instruction explains why the U.S. imposed sanctions against Nicaragua, but not against South Africa. This blatant apology for South Africa spells out, most clearly, the essence of the Reagan Administration policy of constructive engagement.

Finally, it should be quite obvious that the political economy of settler colonialism in South Africa flows from a specific model of capitalist accumulation which is inextricably bound up with the interest and imperatives of imperialist capital. The abolition of apartheid is a direct and immediate threat to imperialist survival.

South Africa had its historical beginnings and will meet its historical end, though as it turns out, its destruction has been an even more tortuous, historic process than its genesis—thanks to the support by imperialism.

NOTES

1. Fifty years ago, South Africa's Minister of Native Affairs addressed Parliament on the San, better known as the Bushmen, a people once numbering 300,000 who have come within a hair's breadth of being exterminated.

   Said the minister: "It would be a biological crime if we allowed this peculiar race to die out, because it is a race that looks more like a baboon than a baboon itself does. So far, we have about 20 that are just about genuine. We intend letting them stay (in a national park as a tourist attraction) and allow them to hunt with bows and arrows, but without dogs. We regard them as part of the fauna of this country." (Quoted in Michael Valpry, "Warped Minds Revealed in Chats," *The Globe and Mail*, Canada [February 1986]:A8.

2. Mark Twain's Connecticut Yankee was expressing the same idea when he said of the productive workers that "They were a nation, the actual Nation; they were about all of it that was useful or worth saving or really respectworthy, and to subtract them would have been to subtract the Nation and leave behind some dregs, some refuse, in the shape of a king, nobility and gentry, idle, unproductive, acquainted mainly with the arts of wasting and destroying and of no sort of use or value in any rationally constructed world." (*A Connecticut Yankee in King Arthur's Court*, with an Afterword by Edmund Reiss, New York: A Signet Classic, 1889, p. 91.) In developing his teaching about productive labor Adam Smith had earlier written that "the labour of menial servants, unproductive in any value. . . . The sovereign, for example, with all the officers of both justice and war who serve under him, the whole army and navy, are unproductive labourers. . . . In the same class must be ranked, some both of the gravest and most important, and some of the most frivolous professions: churchmen, lawyers, physicians, opera-singers, opera-dangers, etc." (*An Inquiry into the Nature and Causes of the Worth of Nations*, Vol. II, London: Basil, 1801, pp. 94-95.)

3. Anthony Trollope, *South Africa: A Report of the 1878 Edition*, with an Introduction and Notes by J.H. Davidson, Cape Town: A.A. Balkema, 1878, pp. 454-462.

4. Trollope, *op. cit.*, p. 45.

5. Lord Bryce, *Impressions on South Africa*, New York: The New American Library, 1969, p. 477.

6. Hugh Tinker, *The New System of Slavery*, London, Oxford University Press, 1974.

7. For example, President Botha said recently, "we are a country of multi-cultural societies. Every one of these multi-cultural societies has certain rights; cultural rights, language rights, a way of life that should be protected. In SA, you do not have a white minority as against a black majority. That is quite a wrong way of looking at things in SA. We have a country of different minorities—a white minority and black minorities" (*Financial Mail*, May 31, 1985). Gavin Relly, President of the Anglo–

American Corporation, spoke of "the number of different constituencies that make up South African society—whites, coloureds, urban blacks, Zulu's, homelands that have achieved a degree of viability and places like Natal where racial integration is already relatively far advanced" (*Ibid.*).

8.   R. Palme Dutt, *The Crisis of Britain and the British Empire*, New York: International Publishers, 1953, pp. 43-44.
9.   On the same point Robinson and Gallagher (1961, 9) write that
     By the Eighteen seventies, confederated Canada, responsibly governed Australasia and the Cape were regarded as constitutional embodiments of collaboration between British and colonial interests working at its best. The further slackening of formal bonds by colonial governments, it is true, raised qualms about the future of imperial unity. Yet the policy-makers felt sure that their self-governing colonials, bound with the silken cords of kindred, tradition and self-interest, would continue to be their most loyal and energetic partners in spreading British influence and multiplying British commerce. Unlike the financial and trading enterprises which were thrusting into Oriental empires, those of the white colonist were proving commercially and politically creative. They had the supreme virtue of being self-propelling. The impetus to expansion was soon coming, not so much from the Metropolis as from the colonial communities themselves.
10. Dutt, *op. cit.*
11. Quoted in V.I. Lenin, *Selected Works*, Vol. I, Moscow: Progress Publishers, 1967, p. 737.
12. Quoted in Lenin, *ibid.*, p. 756.
13. W.E. Stead, in 1902, wrote: "Mr. Rhodes, as I said, is a Darwinian. He believes in the gospel of evolution, of the survival of the fittest, of progress by natural selection. But Mr. Rhodes is not a Chauvinist. He was conducting a serious examination into a supremely important question, and he would take nothing for granted. There are various races of mankind—the Yellow, the Black, the Brown, and the White. If the test be numerical, the Yellow race comes first. But if the test be the area of the world and the power to control its destinies, the primacy of the White race is indisputable. The Yellow race is massed thick on one half of a single continent: the White exclusively occupies Europe, practically occupies the Americas, is colonizing Australia, and is dominating Asia. In the struggle for existence the White race has unquestionably come out on top." (Cecil John Rhodes, *The Last Will and Testament of Cecil John Rhodes, with Elucidatory Notes*, Ed. by W.T. Stead, London: "Review of Reviews" Office, 1902, pp. 92-94.)
14. Bernard Semmel, *Imperialism and Social Reform: English Social-Imperial Thought 1895–1914*, New York: Doubleday, 1960.
15. Stead, *op. cit.*, pp. 58-59.
16. Robert A. Huttenback, *Racism and Empire, White Settlers and Coloured Immigrants in the British Self-Governing Colonies 1830–1910*, Ithaca: Cornell University Press, 1976, p. 18.

17. *Ibid.*, p. 21.
18. *Ibid.*, p. 18.
19. Trollope, *op. cit.*, p. 456.
20. Edward Jessup, *Ernest Oppenheimer: A Study in Power*, London: Rex Collings, 1979, p. 13.
21. Trollope, *op. cit.*, p. 368.
22. *Ibid.*
23. *Ibid.*, p. 369.
24. The Grahamstown "Journal" felt that Trollope was substantially correct when it editorialized that "the welfare of the native races, no less than our own, imperatively demands that we should strive to fit him [the African] for the humble but happy position which he alone is fit to occupy; and not turn his head with nonsensical ideas of his equality with us in internal powers and social rights. Christianity, to be successful with Kafirs, ought to be studied more in connection with spade and shears, saucepan and flat-iron, than with slate and copy-book. . . . Nor do we greatly care to see trade schools established for the natives. Experience does not show that they really practice the trades they are taught in such institutions. . . . If they did, it would be with the result of driving the white man out of the country; for Mr. Trollope concludes from his wide experience that the two classes will not work side by side." Quoted by Davidson in the Introduction to Trollope, *op. cit.*, p. 18.
25. Alexander Wilmot, *The Story of the Expansion of South Africa*, 2nd ed., London, 1895, pp. 2–3.
26. A. Hepple, *South Africa: A Political and Economic History*, New York: Frederick A. Prager, 1966, p. 197.
27. L.S. Stavrianos, *Global Rift: The Third World Comes of Age*, New York: William Morrow and Co., 1981, p. 573.
28. H. Alan C. Cairns, *Prelude to Imperialism: British Reactions to Central African Society 1840–1890*, London: Routledge & Kegan Paul, 1965, p. 238.
29. Shula Marks and Stanley Trapido, "Lord Milner and the South African State," *History Workshop: A Journal of Socialist Historians*, 8 (Autumn 1979):66.
30. As his administrative staff, Sir Alfred (Lord Milner now) gathered round him a group of aides that later became known, half-derisively and half-admiringly, as Milner's Kindergarten. They must have been collectively the most brilliant, practical, and ruthless group of officials ever to serve the British Empire. It is necessary only to mention their names to recognize the political and intellectual caliber of the Kindergarten: there was Philip Kerr, later Lord Lothian; Geoffrey Dawson, later for twenty years the editor of the *Times* of London; Lionel Curtis, later professor of Colonial History at Oxford; John Buchan, the novelist, later Lord Tweedsmuir, the Governor-General of Canada; John Brand, later Lord Brand, the famous banker; Sir Herbert Baker, the famous architect; L.S. Amery, the cabinet minister; Lionel Hitchens; Edward Grigg; Sir Douglas

Malcolm; and Sir Patrick Duncan, later Governor-General of South
Africa. Their ideological beliefs were explained as follows by Milner:
> I have emphasized the importance of the racial bond. From my point of
> view this is fundamental. It is the British race which built the Empire,
> and it is the undivided British race which can alone uphold it . . . deeper,
> stronger, more primordial than these material ties is the bond of
> common blood, a common language, common history and traditions.
> But what do I mean by the British race? I mean all the peoples of the
> United Kingdom and their descendants in other countries under the
> British flag (Quoted by Semmel, *op. cit.*, p. 1733).

31. Eric Habsbawn, *Revolutionaries: Contemporary Essays*, New York: Pantheon
    Books, 1973, p. 123.
32. *Ibid.*, p. 1927.
33. Quoted in Lenin, *op. cit.*, p. 760.
34. British imperial policy in South Africa served to reproduce English class
    relations on an enlarged scale. In the nineteenth century there was a
    frequent comparison made between Africans and the lower classes in
    Britain. Cairns (*op. cit.*, pp. 92-93) writes:
    > For the humanitarian there was a tendency to regard Africans as an
    > external proletariat making a claim on the public conscience comparable
    > to that made by the working classes of Britain. There was the same
    > feeling of paternal or aristocratic responsibility. Both were deprived
    > groups, and therefore both made claims on humanitarian and
    > evangelical sympathies. The working class was at the bottom of the
    > internal class hierarchy and the African was at the bottom of the world
    > cultural and racial hierarchy, a conjunction of low status which
    > encouraged placing the two in the same category. Livingstone, for
    > example, frequently compared the African to the British poor. He
    > asserted that the difference in position between Africans and Britons
    > was as great "as between the lowest and highest in England," and that if
    > he were not a missionary in Africa he would be a missionary of the
    > poor in London. On another occasion he compared himself to "those
    > who perform benevolent deeds at home" and his porters to the "idle
    > and ungrateful poor." Much of the descriptive language was also
    > similar. When Bishop Steere talked of the frightful immorality of
    > village life—"simply incredible"—he was in fact referring to rural
    > England. Burton, after castigating the "sterile" intellect of the East
    > African—"apparently unaggressive and unfit for change"—remarked
    > that "his intelligence is surprising when compared with that of an
    > uneducated English peasant." The significance of this comparison
    > should not be exaggerated, for it was not widely used. Yet if the
    > analogy was seldom conscious, there was a sense in which the
    > humanitarian approach to Africa tended to implicitly assume that
    > Britain as a whole stood in the same relation to Africans as a
    > responsible upper class stood to the lower classes within the

boundaries of the nation. The tendency for race relations to be patterned after class relations was indicated by the frequent assumption that the most important qualities required of those who aspired to positions of influence and control over primitive populations were found in the attributes of a gentleman. The gentleman concept, with its implication that the utilization of power should be suffused with moral purpose and restrained from abuse by inner controls, was, in an African setting, a direct transference of a successful pattern of responsible class behavior within Britain. It was later to reach its apogee in the District Officer whose qualifications were related less to high academic attainments than to the intangibles of character.

35. Stanley J. Stein and Barbara Stein, *The Colonial Heritage of Latin America: Essays on Economic Dependence in Perspective,* New York: Oxford University Press, 1970, p. 57.

36. M. Legassick, "Legislation, Ideology and Economy in Post-1948 South Africa," *Journal of Southern African Studies,* Vol. I (1974):32-33.

37. H.J. Simons and Ray Simons, *Class and Colour in South Africa, 1850–1950,* Baltimore: Penguin, 1967, p. 623.

38. Jack Barnes, "The Coming Revolution in South Africa," *New International,* 2.2 (1985):14.

39. Romero Daniels, "To Maggie, Sanctions on S.A. is like Self-Strangulation," *The Sunday Mail,* Harare, July 27, 1986, p. C7.

40. Barrington Moore, Jr., *Social Origins of Dictatorship and Democracy: Lord and Peasant in the Making of the Modern World,* Boston: Beacon Press, 1967, p. 433.

41. *Ibid.*

42. *Ibid.*

43. Frederick Johnstone, Review of Alan Jeeves, *Migrant Labour in South Africa,* In *Labour, Capital and Society,* 18.2 (1985):422.

44. Karl Marx, *The German Ideology,* ed. by C.J. Arthur, New York: International Publishers, 1970, p. 146.

45. Jessup, *op. cit.,* p. 3. Further, S. Arronovitch (*The Ruling Classes: A Study of British Finance Capital,* London: Lawrence and Wishart, 1961, p. 43), in explaining the complex ways in which fusion is brought about between banking and corporate capital and industrial capital, writes:

   Rhodes—in developing the South African gold mines and in forming the Chartered Company of British South Africa, turned to and received help from the Rothschilds in return for a continuing stake in South African gold, diamonds, uranium and other resources. At a later stage in building up the Anglo–American Corporation of South Africa, Sir Ernest Oppenheimer turned to [the] Morgans of American who invested substantially.

46. Ernest Chamberlain, the British Colonial Secretary, prior to the beginning of the Anglo-Boer War (1900–1902), recognized the centrality of the gold mines for the future of South Africa and planned accordingly:

I shall never go into such a war with a light heart, and at the present time we have no reason—either of right or interest—which would justify the enterprise.

If we would be forced into it against our will I should try to seize and defend the gold bearing districts. This is the key of S. Africa and if we could hold this we need not follow the Boers into the wilderness. (Ronald Robinson and John Gallagher, with Alice Denny, *Africa and the Victorians: The Climax of Imperialism*, New York: Anchor Books, 1961, p. 432.)

47. S.H. Pyrah, *Imperial Policy in South Africa, 1902–1910*, London: Oxford University Press, 1955, p. 37.
48. R.W. Johnson, *How Long Will South Africa Survive?*, New York: Oxford University Press, 1977, p. 67.
49. Karl Marx, *Capital*, Vol. III, New York: International Publishers, 1967, pp. 791-792.
50. *Ibid.*
51. Simons & Simons, *op. cit.*, p. 42.
52. Karl Marx, *Capital*, Vol. I, New York: International Publishers, 1967, p. 863.
53. Herbert S. Frankel, *Capital Investment in Africa*, London: Oxford University Press, 1938, p. 52.
54. Hance, William A., *The Geography of Modern Africa*, New York: Columbia University Press, 1964, p. 523.
55. *Newsweek*, December 16, 1974, p. 82.
56. Duncan Innes, *Anglo-American and the Rise of a Modern South Africa*, New York: Monthly Review Press, 1973, p. 70.
57. Pallo Z. Jordan, *Socialist Transformation and the Freedom Charter*, Lusaka, Zambia, The ANC Research Unit, 1983, p. 3.
58. Quoted in Johnson, *op. cit.*, p. 85.
59. Jordan, *op. cit.*,
60. *The Nation Magazine*, November 22, 1986, pp. 538-539.

4

Socialist Transformation and the Freedom Charter

Z. Pallo Jordan

This conference, whose theme is "Socialist Transformation in South Africa," comes at a time when our entire region is seized by the problem of a well-orchestrated counterrevolutionary drive directed from Pretoria. To some it may appear ironic that it is at this time that the social scientists of southern Africa have chosen to address themselves to this theme when the radical transformations that have occurred during the last decade are manifestly in danger. The irony, however, is not that great when one recalls that to one extent or another the changes that so dramatically changed the geopolitics of our subcontinent were all inspired by precisely the vision of "Socialist Transformation." Indeed, the counterrevolution is directed specifically against this cutting edge.

We are meeting also during 1983, the 100th anniversary of the death of Karl Marx, one of the founders of scientific socialism, who during his lifetime made the most prolific and profound contribution to the theory of socialist transformation. Marx's writings are indeed wide-ranging, covering many different countries, representing various forms of political and economic domination. Though this paper will deal specifically with South Africa, and will be addressing itself to the manner in which South African revolutionaries, partisans of the national liberation movement, have approached this question, and will attempt to outline the theory of the South African Revolution that has evolved from these approaches, we shall be drawing on the particularly rich heritage bequeathed to humanity by Marx and his co-worker, Engels. The writings of Marx and Engels on colonialism, the national question, and the struggle for democracy, have a particular relevance for South Africa in the present day. Many of these, we feel, can assist us in throwing light on some of the more thorny problems of theory and revolutionary practice that confront our country and its people.

A comparison of the map of Europe, east of the Rhine, during the 1840s when Marx first entered politics, and South Africa today, clearly demonstrates the relevance of Marx's work to the problems that beset our country in the present day.

Both maps, on examination, would reveal an extraordinary degree of fragmentation, an immense disparity in the sizes of the various fragments and the levels of socio-economic development both within and among the fragments. What the observer would have to discover are the political realities behind the map: birth pangs caused by a new social and political order struggling to emerge. He would observe also, hidden behind that map, two apparently contradictory yet integrally related processes: the dismemberment of an empire(s) and the unification of nations.

Nineteenth-century Europe and southern Africa during the last quarter of the twentieth century are qualitatively different situations, we can hear our readers object. And we have to agree. But, let us focus our attention on one of these similarities for a moment to bring out the parallels we are referring to.

Speaking at the Fourth Congress of the Frelimo Party, Comrade President O.R. Tambo said of the ANCs vision of our country's future:

> We conceive of our country as a single, united, democratic and non-racial state, belonging to all who live in it, in which all shall enjoy equal rights, and in which sovereignty will come from the people as a whole, and not from a collection of Bantustans and racial tribal groups organised to perpetuate minority power.[1]

Compare this with the first two clauses of the "Demands of the Communist Party in Germany" drawn up by Marx and Engels soon after the outbreak of the 1848 Revolution:

> 1.   The whole of Germany shall be declared a single and indivisible republic,

2.   Every German, having reached the age of 21, shall have the right to vote and to be elected, provided he has not been convicted of a criminal offence.[2]

The similarities are striking. But these similarities are not the result of plagiarism on our part. They are, we contend, the outcome of similarities in the circumstances which led to the adoption of common solutions. An even more instructive parallel emerges when we focus on the relations between the Polish and German national movements of the period. Compare the words of Engels on the Polish question:

We German democrats present here clasp hands with the Polish democrats, so the whole German people will celebrate the alliance with the Polish people on the very field of the first battle won in common.[3]

Compare these words with those of President Tambo on Namibia:

The ANC once again affirms its support for the people of Namibia in their legitimate struggle for national independence under the leadership of SWAPO. The apartheid regime must be encircled by your struggles and by your actions; by our struggles and by our actions. Together with you we shall be unconquerable and invincible.[4]

DECAYING FEUDALISM AND MONOPOLY CAPITALISM

Though there are these parallels between Europe of the 1840s and South Africa of the present, we do not intend that these be carried too far. More important and illuminating are the divergences in the two situations.

Europe, east of the Rhine, during the 1840s represented a stark picture of decaying feudalism, overripe for the bourgeois democratic revolution. This state of sociopolitical putrefaction rested on the twin pillars of the counterrevolutionary compact concluded in Vienna at the close of the Napoleonic Wars, and the political flabbiness of the big bourgeoisie of these territories, especially Germany. One regional power, Tsarist Russia, underwrote and sustained these obsolete institutions with its armed might.

The German bourgeoisie's fear was occasioned not by its economic backwardness or weakness but precisely by its strength. Within the confines of the archaic institutions of absolutism, the bourgeoisie had accumulated wealth, established factories, and had even forced a half-hearted type of land reform on the landowning Junkers. These developments, however, produced their historical concomitant, the proletariat, which, though still in its infancy, had demonstrated its revolutionary potential and embraced political ambitions and a social vision the bourgeoisie might find impossible to contain. The images of Jacques Roux, the Enrages, not to mention Babeouf, were still fresh in the minds of the European bourgeoisie. They therefore chose to deal with the devil they knew rather than entertain the risky project of arousing the masses to revolutionary struggle. Commenting on this turn of events, Marx wrote:

> The German bourgeoisie developed so sluggishly, timidly and slowly that at the moment it menacingly confronted feudalism and absolutism, it saw menacingly confronting it the proletariat and all sections of the middle class whose interests and ideas were related to those of the proletariat. . . . from the first the German bourgeoisie was inclined to betray the people and to compromise with the crowned representative of the old society, for it itself already belonged to the old society. . . . The big bourgeoisie, which was all along anti-revolutionary, concluded a defensive and offensive alliance with the reactionary forces, because it was afraid of the people, i.e. of the workers and the democratic bourgeoisie.[5]

The abandonment of revolution by the bourgeoisie imposed on Marx and Engels the task of reevaluating the whole character of the revolution in Germany. They concluded that a new type of bourgeois revolution was in the making in which the task of mobilizing and leading the other revolutionary forces devolved on the proletariat, since the bourgeoisie had ceased being revolutionary.

The German bourgeois democrats and socialists had conceived of the national democratic revolution as entailing two inseparable processes: the unification of the German people, to include those of Austria and those of the smaller German principalities, on the one hand; and the emancipation of the various smaller nations oppressed by Austrian and Prussian absolutism, on the other hand. In contrast to them, the forces of reaction in both Prussia and Austria, for divergent reasons, were opposed to the unification of the German people. Prussia, the weaker of the two, though favoring unification under its domination, realistically could not support it since it could lead to Austrian domination over Prussia. Austria too would have preferred unification under Austrian control but feared that advocacy of national rights might have a subversive effect on its non-German dependencies. The Austrians therefore became proponents of confederation because this would enable them to dominate the other German states while retaining their oppressive grip on the smaller nations within the Hapsburg Empire.

The upshot was that Germany's transition to full-fledged capitalism was presided over by a Bonapartist regime headed by Bismarck and the military caste of Prussia. Austria was excluded from this unified Germany and wars of conquest rather than revolutionary struggle, initiated from below, became the chief agency of sociopolitical change. The tragic consequences of this evolution do not form part of our theme and have been widely discussed elsewhere.

In sharp contrast to the decaying feudalism of nineteenth-century Europe, South Africa today is a highly integrated capitalist socioeconomic formation characterized by the domination of huge industrial, financial, and mining monopolies. Yet we find that the country is being fragmented and subdivided into various ethnic and racial compartments. All fractions of the ruling monopoly capitalist class—to different degrees—advocate the creation of artificial ministates and tribal principalities as a bulwark against revolutionary change from below.

Fearful that any popularly-initiated change of the political order may have consequences inimical to their property rights, the very class whose historical task was once described as becoming "political centralization" almost daily concocts harebrained schemes—"federalism, confederalism, consociationism, national pluralism"—anything but the unitary state, as a means of preserving white minority domination and capitalist power under some superficially "new" guise. In the most obscene and absurd imitation of the white capitalist interests groups they serve, various black collaborationist leaders have offered up their versions in the shape of ethnic utopias, the so-called "Buthelezi Commission," and a host of other farcical proposals.

The National Liberation Movement has thus emerged as the only champion of democracy and national unity. Consistent with these principles, the ANC is also the only consistent ally and advocate of the national emancipation of the Namibian people under the leadership of their vanguard, SWAPO. We have here again the recapitulation of the tasks Marx and Engels assigned to the new democratic movement, headed by the proletariat of Europe more than 150 years ago.

THE EVOLUTION OF A THEORY OF THE SOUTH AFRICAN REVOLUTION
The South African liberation movement, headed by the ANC, is a

multiclass alliance embracing movements that draw their inspiration from two modern political currents, nationalism and socialism. Though South Africa is not unique in this respect, there is one dimension of our movement which was not present in others of this region; namely, the presence of an organized Marxist-Leninist party as a component of the liberation movement. African Nationalism in South Africa traces its origins to the liberal-democratic traditions of the European "Enlightenment," imbibed by the mission-educated African petit-bourgeoisie. Socialism came to our country in the baggage of European immigrant workers and returning black students who had been exposed to the influences of the labor movement in Europe. The complex interaction between these two currents in our movement has been dealt with elsewhere. We shall focus here on how these two grew together, leading first to a political alliance and later to the emergence of a common approach to the immediate tasks facing our people and our country. To elucidate this process we shall discuss separately the various approaches that have evolved within these two traditions.

African nationalism in South Africa can be dated from the first half of the nineteenth century, when two black converts, Jan Tshatshu and Andries Stoffels, travelled to Britain as part of a missionary-led deputation to petition the British colonial authorities. Both were representatives of the "new men" who had come into existence in the interstices between European colonizer and the African colonized. Attracted by the achievements of European thought and technique, the new men oscillated between collaboration and resistance. Unlike the majority of their countrymen, they were modernists, seeking to master the instruments of European culture and the political institutions created by the colonialists in the Cape. At the same time, they were repelled by the brutal aggression of the British and the racial arrogance of the colonialists. In the end, both Tshatshu and Stoffels finally opted for resistance.

It was only after 1880 that a large enough number of blacks with access to the political institutions of the Cape came into being. Before this time meaningful participation in Cape politics had not been possible. Organized black politics is usually dated from this period, which saw the first mass registration of African voters and the publication of the first secular newspapers in the African languages (1884). The following three decades constitute the formative years of African political thought during which African political leaders were forced to adapt to and learn from the changing needs of Cape liberalism and the shifting policies of the British imperialists. The inauguration of the Union of South Africa in 1910 brings this period to a close.

The founding of the ANC in January 1912 marks the end, but also the beginning, of a political practice that had developed among the black elite over the last decades of the nineteenth century. It brought to a close the preceding period during which black politics had been concerned with fighting an unsuccssful rearguard action in defense of the few rights the black petit-bourgeoisie had enjoyed under colonial rule, but it was also the beginning of a new era during which black politics would increasingly challenge the institutions of white over-lordship and in the process learn to pose alternatives and new options for the country as a whole. In this light the conception of the ANC as an alternative parliament, so often decried as puerile mimicry of the British ruling class, was itself a revolutionary measure. As the "parliament of the African people," the ANC assumed the role of custodian of ideals, aspirations, and political values that had no place in the "official" white parliament. Implicit in these actions was the intent to seize the initiative from the white minority and reshape the entire body politic to their own design.

The European liberal tradition formed the core ideas of the politics of the national movement during its early years. These were the ideas the leadership had learned from their predecessors. They shared an idealized perception of the British Empire and its institutions, all supposedly rooted in this political tradition. That the empire was in reality a prison house for millions of Africans and Asians escaped their notice. They, like their white counterparts therefore, turned to Britain as the final arbiter in South African affairs and tried to legitimize their claims by an appeal to this political tradition. It was of course the economic realities—rich mines, large farms, the need for a mass labor force—that carried weight in Whitehall. Hence it was the pro-imperialism white settler bourgeoisie and its Afrikaner nationalist opponents who received a sympathetic hearing in London.

The political programs and objectives of both these latter dovetailed with the interest of British imperialism. African nationalism did not. Thus, despite the skeleton of the Boer republican rebellion rattling in his political cupboard, General Hertzog was able to secure a firm promise for greater autonomy when he went to London at the end of World War I in 1918. The African nationalists, who had loyally stood by the Empire and enthusiastically mobilized volunteers for the Native Labour Contingent, came back empty-handed.

The racial exclusivity of the Union constitution, however, also had a quite unintended effect. Racism circumscribed the activities of the black elite in the state, the economy, and the political and cultural institutions into dealing mainly with their own people. This tended to reinforce group cohesion and solidarity, both of which became factors in political action. Confined to the ghetto of its skin color, the elite also became susceptible to aspirations and objectives that were not necessarily its own. It gradually came to realize that the fulfilment, even of its own limited objectives and ambitions, was contingent upon the status of the black community as a whole. This realization imposed on it the task of acting as the spokesman of the Africans and other oppressed nationalities.

As Thomas Hodgkin has noted, every African colonial city was divided into an opulent white section and an impoverished African section, which stimulated an identification with socially radical causes. The legal racial barriers erected to hold back black advancement made it plain that the distribution of wealth, power, and privilege was not preordained, but was the direct consequence of a particular mode of organization of the economic and political order. The intransigence of the white ruling class, the vacillation and betrayal of principles by erstwhile friends in the liberal establishment, and the growing capacity for struggle displayed by the poorer strata of the black population, all had a radicalizing impact on the black elite which synchronized with its own changing self-perception.

The most important contributory factor to the radicalization of black politics, specifically that of the ANC, was the impact of industrial development. This catalyzed the emergence of a rapidly-growing black urban community, made up overwhelmingly of industrial workers who had acquired a stake in life within the modern sector of the economy. It was from among these that the first mass black trade union, the Industrial and Commercial Workers Union of Africa (ICU), developed during the 1920s.

Starting out as a dockworkers' union on the Cape Town waterfront, the ICU grew into a nationwide general workers' union which at the peak of its power had a membership of over 100,000 unskilled African and colored workers. The inflow of politicized black workers, many of whom received their political initiation in the ICU, into the ANC during the 1920s was bound to have a radicalizing effect. That these events coincided with the presidency of Josiah T. Gumede was both a fortunate coincidence and its effect.

Josiah T. Gumede's political evolution is itself very instructive about the radicalization we are referring to. He started as a devout Christian and committed liberal, violently opposed to what he saw as the pernicious influence of the communists among the African working class. By 1926, at the emergency conference convened to discuss Hertzog's Native Administration Bill, he emerged as the leading spokesman of the radical minority caucus, composed mainly of

younger men, calling for more radical measures—other than petitioning and deputations—to meet the racist regime's onslaught. It is
generally agreed that the decisive step came when he attended the
World Congress of the League Against Imperialism, held in Brussels in
1927. His report to the ANC's national conference in June of that year
contributed to his election as president. But it is also evident that his
radical views coincided with the mood of the general membership
when we recall that Eddie Khaile, a known communist, was elected as
secretary-general by the same national conference. Though it is difficult to document the specific contribution of Gumede and Khaile's
leadership to the evolution of ANC policy because of the scarcity of
primary sources, the few that are extant indicate that they introduced a
revolutionary new theme into ANC politics.

Before June 1927, it would be fair to describe the ANC's strategy and
the political outlook of its leadership as liberal-reformist. The notion of
overthrowing white minority domination and replacing it with a
government representative of the majority was at best considered
utopian, at worst the scheme of wild-eyes extremists. The aims of the
ANC, as expressed in the "African Bill of Rights," adopted in 1923
were:

1. The restoration of the Cape African Franchise and its
   extension to the other provinces (i.e., a property-owner
   franchise)
2. The abolition of the statutory color bar
3. Restoration of the African rights to buy and sell land
   anywhere in the country

In other words, the struggle was conceived of as essentially a struggle
for civil rights, an extension to the blacks of the rights enjoyed by the
whites within the framework of the 1910 Union constitution. As for the
idea of radically restructuring the economy, that was not even part of
their political vocabulary.

The clearest exposition of the political strategy and program
associated with the Gumede-Khaile leadership of 1927–30 is contained
in Gumede's presidential address to the ANC's annual conference in
April 1930. It was, ironically, this address that precipitated his removal
from the presidency. This should hardly be surprising if we bear in
mind that this was the first explicit call for majority rule emanating
from a sub-Saharan liberation movement in the period preceding the
Second World War. Gumede's radicalism frightened the ANC old
guard, reared on the politics of moderation and "respectful petitioning."

The most radical departure was in the area of strategy. Gumede called upon the oppressed to unite and rely on their own organized strength rather than on the empty promises and doubtful loyalties of the liberal establishment. The tactics of deputations and petitioning had proved fruitless, the regime would only respond to power . . . and that lay in the numbers of the oppressed and the dependence of the economy on their labor power.

Though the movement had been conceived as the political home of all the African people, it has in fact mainly struck root among the educated elite in the rural areas and the most acculturated and urbanized among the urban Africans. The outlook of the leadership and the tactics it employed reflected this rather narrow political base. The influx of workers into the movement was beginning to change all that. Having been called into the political arena by the predominantly petit-bourgeois leadership, the black working class was acquiring objectives of its own, which it could, in time, impose on the movement as a whole because of its numerical strength. The political implications of such a strategy were clear to a number of the old guard of the ANC. If accepted, it would hasten this process and thus take matters out of the hands of the elite.

Gumede also introduced a new dimension into the ANC's self-image. From its inception, the ANC had a Pan-African vision, embracing the whole continent and peoples of African descent in the new world. Gumede now sought to extend this by making references to the Asian struggles for liberation, establishing a community of interests based not only on skin color and geography, but principally on common struggle against imperialism. The strategy of the ANC, as he saw it, would embrace these two aspects as its primary thrust—the self-emancipation of the oppressed black people and the solidarity of the anti-imperialist and anticolonial forces.

As the immediate program towards which to strive, Gumede broke completely with the reformist tradition. His premise was the illegitimacy of the white racist regime. From this it followed that what was required was not a rearrangement of its parts but a completely new structure. This was expressed in the call for a "Black Republic" as the ANC's central political demand. It was this that proved to be the last straw for the old guard. Though he did not spell out the institutional framework of this "Black Republic," it is clear that it necessarily entailed majority rule and the creation of political institutions of popular power as a condition and guarantor of majority rule.

Led by Seme, Mahabane, and Mapikela, the old guard leadership campaigned to have Gumede ousted from the presidency and restored the prior state of affairs with a vengeance. In areas like the Cape Province, a McCarthyite-style witchhunt was conducted to drive Gumede's working-class supporters out of the ANC. The revolutionary nationalism he espoused, however, survived as an underground current within the movement, reappearing during the 1940s when a new generation of fighters rediscovered it.

THE REVOLUTIONARY NATIONALIST TRADITION

It took the national liberation movement almost ten years to recover from the disastrous consequences of the purge of the radicals. During the 1940s, the main exponents of a radial approach to politics were the ANC Youth League (ANCYL).

At its founding congress, the ANCYL announced that it adhered to the ideology of African nationalism, that it saw itself as the "brains trust and power station" of this ideology within the ANC whose objective was to transform the movement into a broad-based movement fighting for national freedom and the unity of the African people.

The principles of African nationalism, as understood by the ANCYL, are set forth in one of its founding documents, *The Youth League Manifesto:*[6]

- That the African people, like any other people, have the "inalienable right to national self-determination"
- That the emancipation of the African people "will be achieved by the Africans themselves"
- That the leadership of the ANC "must be the personification of the aspirations of the people"

We can note in these the continuities between the thinking of the ANCYL leaders and the radicals of the 1920s. These were to be the most enduring contributions of these two groups to the evolution of ANC strategy and tactics. We may note the following themes:

1. White supremacy, no matter in what guise, is essentially illegitimate.
2. The oppressed people claim the right to national self-determination—i.e., racist South Africa cannot be considered a sovereign state.
3. The oppressed people must be their own liberators.
4. Since power will not be willingly conceded, the need [is] to employ whatever means are necessary to wrest power from the white minority regime.

It was on the initiative of the ANCYL that the ANC adopted the famous Programme of Action of 1949,[7] whose preamble states:

> The fundamental principles of the Programme of Action . . . are inspired by the desire to achieve National Freedom. By National Freedom we mean freedom from White domination and the attainment of political independence. This implies the rejection of the conception of segregation, apartheid, trusteeship, or White leadership which are all motivated by the idea of White domination. . . .

The implications latent in Gumede's earlier call for reliance on the organized strength of the oppressed were translated into reality after the Programme of Action was adopted in 1949. The 1950s saw the transformation of the ANC into a mass political movement leading and initiating popular campaigns, strikes, and civil disobedience campaigns during what we know as the "fighting fifties."

Neither in the perspectives propounded by Gumede nor in those of the Youth League was there an acknowledgement of the need to pass beyond the National Democratic Revolution. True, specific individuals like Khaile, associated with both, espoused such causes. How do we then include these developments as significant to the theme "Socialist Transformation?"

To answer this question we have recourse once more to the work of the founders of scientific socialism. Referring to the Polish question, Engels in a letter addressed to Karl Kautsky during 1882, says among other things:

> It is historically impossible for a large people to discuss seriously any internal question as long as its national independence is lacking. . . . To get rid of national oppression is the basic condition of all healthy free movement. . . .[8]

We as a movement, concurring with Engels, would insist that the seizure of political power is the essential element of any social change in South Africa.

The significance of the tradition pioneered by Gumede and Khaile, later built on and developed by the ANCYL leaders, lies in its contribution to the theory of the national democratic revolution. But before we can pass over into the present phase, it is necessary to trace the other political tradition that has inspired our liberation alliance.

THE MARXIST TRADITION

In their writings on colonialism, Marx and Engels bring to light two contradictory yet integrally related tendencies in colonialism. This was first expressed by Marx with reference to India:

> England has to fulfil a double mission in India; one destructive the other regenerating—the annihilation of old Asiatic society, and to lay the material foundation of Western society in Asia.[9]

However, always keenly aware of the duality of all historical processes, Marx also recorded the human cost of this regenerating role: "England has broken down the entire framework of Indian society, without any symptoms of reconstitution yet appearing. This loss of his old world, with no gain of a new one, imparts a particular kind of melancholy to the present misery of the Hindu. . . ."[10]

In laying the "material foundations of Western society in Asia," the colonialists were, however, unconsciously performing their historical task which would have consequences they had neither planned nor anticipated:

> I know that the English millocracy intend to endow India with railways with the exclusive view of extracting at diminished expenses the cotton and other raw materials for their manufactures. But when you have once introduced machinery into the locomotion of a country, which possesses iron and coal, you are unable to withold it from its fabrication. You cannot maintain a net of railways over an immense country without introducing all those industrial processes necessary to meet the immediate and current wants of railway locomotion, and out of which there must grow the application of machinery to those branches of industry not immediately connected with railways.[11]

Because of this, Marx concludes: "Whatever may have been the crimes of England, she was the unconscious tool of history. . . ."[12]

These unintended consequences of colonialism were nonetheless realities which Marx and Engels anticipated would shake Asia out of its torpor and bring it abreast of developments in Europe and North America. But the Indians would never really derive the full benefit of this social revolution until

> . . . in Great Britain itself the now ruling classes shall have been

> supplanted by the industrial proletariat, or till the Hindus
> themselves shall have grown strong enough to throw off the
> English yoke altogether.[13]

It was specifically in relation to Ireland that Marx and Engels were able to study the effects of colonialism at close quarters and began to define a revolutionary strategy for relating the anticolonial national struggles to the working class struggles in the metropolitan countries. As we can see above, Marx at one time hoped that a successful working class movement in Britain would be able to extend national independence to the colonies. The militancy of the Chartist movement during the 1840s and 1850s reinforced these hopes. By 1869, in a letter addressed to Engels, Marx was forced by events to revise his earlier assessment.

> For a long time I believed that it would be possible to overthrow
> the Irish regime by English working class ascendancy. . . . Deeper
> study has convinced me of the opposite. The English working
> class will never accomplish anything before it has got rid of
> Ireland. The lever must be applied in Ireland.[14]

From this followed the conclusion that it was the task of the British working class to support the Irish independence movement both as a deserving cause in itself and as an essential condition for their own emancipation from capital. Marx in these writings begins to draw linkages between the colonial revolution and the struggle for socialism. In relation to the Irish movement in particular Marx stressed that these two fronts of struggle are mutually dependent.

The destructive regenerative aspects of colonialism have perhaps been nowhere more evident than in South Africa itself where British imperialism pulverized the precapitalist African societies in order to make room for the most far-reaching social revolution yet experienced in Africa. In a matter of a few generations, the people of South Africa were force-marched from early communalism into the epoch of monopoly capitalism. The mining revolution of the 1880s marks the watershed of South African economic history which saw the implantation of the capitalist mode of production and the transformation of erstwhile traditional peasants into a bonded, mass labor force, press-ganged into the service of capital by taxation and land hunger. But, as Marx had predicted, the South African proletariat, forged in the crucible of these barbarities and tempered in the heat of bitter class struggles, is demonstrating with each passing day its capacity to undertake the profound historical task of leading South Africa to freedom.

Before the First World War, though there were a number of socialists in South Africa, none of them had really addressed themselves to the national question in our country. The split in the South African Labour Party, precipitated by the outbreak of war, led indirectly to the first halting steps in this direction taken by the International Socialist League (ISL) in 1915. Adherence to the principles of internationalism was the basic distinction separating the left from the right wing in South African socialism at the outbreak of the war. The left, as constituted in the ISL, established links with the Zimmerwaldists and were among the first to hail the October Revolution. When the Communist International met in 1919, they immediately sought affiliation. The ISL's identification with Soviet Russia was to have a profound effect on the whole course of the Communist movement's subsequent history, eventually introducing another crucial distinction between official "social democracy" and Marxism-Leninism in South Africa—solidarity with the national liberation movement.

Though the left-laborites who constituted the ISL considered themselves Marxists, they were not particularly well-schooled in Marxism and were completely unfamiliar with the Marxian tradition relating to the national and colonial question. The embryonic South African Communist movement had developed in the peculiar environment of the white immigrant working class struggles in the Witwatersrand and the port cities of South Africa. It was strongly influenced by syndicalism and conceived of the class struggles in terms closely related to what is today referred to as "workerism." Consequently they simply regarded the black workers as the allies of the white workers and ignored the national aspirations of the black workers as members of an oppressed race. They proceeded from the premise that national differences were a device employed by the capitalist class to weaken working class solidarity and therefore should either be ignored or played down.

This attitude also dominated their approach to the national movement led by the black petit-bourgeoisie. In their view this was an elitist pressure group aimed at securing petit-bourgeois sectional interests at the expense of the workers of all races. The pro-imperialist pronouncements of the national leaders of the time only reinforced this view. The Communists' understanding of the South African struggle was put to a profound test barely six months after the founding of the Communist Party of South Africa (CPSA, July 1921) when the whole white working class on the Witwatersrand rose in rebellion in defense of the color bar. This forced a major rethinking of the entire strategy of the South African communist movement and led to the resolution to concentrate on the black working class, sponsored by Bunting at the 1924 annual conference.

The CPSA's turn to the black working class was not merely a reflex to the reverses suffered in 1922, but represented a courageous attempt to deal creatively with the new developments in industry brought about by the war. By 1924, the black industrial working class, called into existence by the growth of secondary industry during the war years, had chalked up a series of stirring mass struggles beginning with the 1918 Bucket Strike in Johannesburg and culminating in the closure of 21 Rand mines during the miners' strike of 1920. The phenomenal growth of the ICU, reflecting the development of a national and class consciousness among the black workers, also laid to rest the racist conception that blacks were incapable of sustained struggle. Alone among the white socialists, the founders of the CPSA recognized the possibility these developments held out and tried to devise policies to unify the racially diverse working class. After 1924 the CPSA was the only political party in South Africa that sought to appeal to all races.

In approaching the national question in South Africa, the CPSA leaned on the experience of the Russian Revolution. The relationship between the revolutionary working class movement and the oppressed nationalities in the Tsarist empire had been the subject of intense debate from the inception of the RSDLP. Though most of the theoretical debate revolved around the Russian dependencies in the west (Poland, the Ukraine, etc.), the principles evolved in relation to these were held to be generally applicable. After the seizure of power by the proletariat in the leading urban and industrial centers of the empire, the pursuance of these principles yielded mixed results. Exercising their right to secede from the dominant Russian nation, former dependencies in the west opted for independence and promptly became springboards for the counterrevolution and interventionists. In the east, the knowledge that the formerly dominant nation had no interest in oppressing them helped to draw the oppressed nationalities to the new Soviet government. This seemed to bear out the essential rectitude of the Bolshevik policy on the national question, despite the disappointments in the west.

The results of the implementation of the Bolshevik nationalities policy could be traced to the specific features of the Russian Empire. Three-quarters of the empire was backward—a sea of peasants, as one writer expressed it—while in a few urban pockets, all of them west of the Urals, some of the largest industrial concentrations employing some of the most advanced industrial plants and productive methods, constituted islands of modernity. It was the revolutionary movement, based in these industrial portions of the empire, that overthrew Tsarism and later the provisional government, thus creating the political space for the western dependencies to secede and the eastern dependencies to choose voluntary association with the new Soviet power. In this respect, the living experience of the Russian revolution seemed to bear out the relationship anticipated in the writings of Marx—the national emancipation of the colonial peoples as a by-product of working-class ascendancy in the metropole.

This idea, the liberation of the colonies from without as a byproduct of socialist revolutions in the advanced capitalist countries, was in fact written into the Communist International's first manifesto to the workers of the world. It was only at the Second Congress of the Comintern that Lenin finally repudiated the concept of the derivative colonial emancipation.

The early South African Communists mechanically transposed the lessons of the Russian experience to the South African setting. The apparent endorsement of this idea by the Comintern in 1919 probably reinforced its legitimacy in the eyes of many. Assuming that the South African revolution would follow the same path as the Russian, the CPSA regarded the white working class as the leading force in the South African revolution which would on its victory "concede the fullest rights which the native working class is capable of claiming."[15]

In keeping with this conception of the South African revolution, the CPSA, while cultivating ties with the black working class, was keen to retain and preserve its roots among the organized white working class. The events of 1922 indicated that it would be difficult to straddle this divide. It took many years for the revolutionary left to grasp the centrality of the national question to any project of a South African revolution.

THE SIXTH CONGRESS OF THE COMINTERN

The Sixth World Congress of the Comintern was spread over a number of weeks during which the colonial and national questions were thoroughly reviewed by the International Communist Movement. In many respects, this congress was the culmination of a process which began during the Second Congress when Lenin decisively broke with the tradition that regarded the colonial countries as mere auxiliaries in the ranks of the world revolution. The keynote address and reports on the colonial question were delivered by Palmiro Togliatti of the Italian

Communist Party, and the Finish Communist, Otto Kuusinen. Togliatti's report was a scathing critique of the colonial policy of the Second International, which had met in conference a few weeks previously.

The report elaborated the repudiation of the notion that colonial freedom would be the byproduct of socialist revolution in the metropolitan countries. This had been a widely-held view in the Second International, even before the First World War. It was based on the assumption, Togliatti held, that the colonial peoples were either incapable or unwilling to free themselves. The political effect of such ideas, the actual intent of their authors notwithstanding, was to give unwitting support to imperialism by reinforcing racist and chauvinist attitudes within the European working class. Most importantly, the report drew attention to the crucial distinctions between capital accumulation as it had occurred in the metropolitan countries and the process taking place in the colonies. According to Togliatti's account, because the colonies were not self-governing, even when sectors of the economy were developed, they had no means of regulating the inflow and outflow of capital and profits. The imperialists had devised a number of policies to perpetuate their domination of the colonies. In some instances, as in India, after defeating the forces of feudalism, the imperialists entered into alliance with them as a means of holding down the aspirant bourgeoisie. In others, the colonial power imposed its own regime and sponsored a comprador-collaborationist stratum while stifling the emergence of an indigenous coalition of classes that would develop a spirit of independence. Lastly, there were the cases where the colonialists prevented the coalescence of a proto-bourgeois class by expropriating the people of their land and handing it to white settlers (as in Algeria, Rhodesia, and Kenya).

The forms of cultivation pursued by the colonialists, large plantations which often resulted in monoculture, visited untold violence on the soil so that countries once renowned for their crops periodically suffered crop failures. Galloping rates of rural impoverishment, all the more painful in the absence of the compensatory development of industry that could absorb the destitute peasants, had become almost universal in the colonial countries, the report charged.

Togliatti's report was to have a profound impact on the colonial liberation movement, imparting to the concept of national self-determination a wider meaning, which would encompass not only political independence, but also economic independence to be achieved through an agrarian revolution and national reconstruction through the creation of an indigenous industrial base. In the countries dominated by white settlers, such an agrarian revolution would entail the expropriation of the settlers; stating the matter unequivocally, Togliatti said: "The natives had been robbed of their land by the Whites. The agrarian revolution, therefore, will have as its chief point in almost all colonial countries the seizure from the Whites of the land which they have stolen."[16]

In regard to South Africa, the congress adopted the famous "Black Republic" resolution as part of a larger resolution on the "Negro Question." Read in relation to the Congress reports by Togliatti and Kuusinen, the section of the resolution dealing with South Africa is greatly illuminating. In 1930 an elaborated version of the resolution adopted in 1928 was published. This was the clearest exposition of a Marxist-Leninist approach to the South African revolution.

The Black Republic Resolution of 1930 characterized South Africa as a British dominion of the colonial type, its central feature being the dispossession of the indigenous people of the land. The main content of the revolution in South Africa therefore was the restoration of the land to the indigenous people. In the national liberation struggle the principal revolutionary agent would be the African peasants, in alliance and under the leadership of the proletariat. The resolutions then pose a number of strategic tasks, the first of which is the development of an alliance between the Communist Party and the national liberation movement. To be effective, the thesis argued, the national movement must base itself on the peasants, the semi-proletariat, and the proletariat. The radical impact of an organized peasant and worker contingent on the national movement would itself lend it a more profound social vision which would bring it into conflict with the less ambitious projects of the state-appointed chiefs. As the workers and peasants acquired self-confidence, their independent political action would also undermine the ideological domination of the national movement by the petit-bourgeois intellectuals.

The principal enemy was identified as British imperialism and the white settler bourgeoisie. A sharp distinction was drawn between the exploiter classes and the white wage-earners, whom the thesis regarded as potential allies of the national revolutionary movement. It stressed however that black and white unity could not be based on pandering to white chauvinism; South Africa was first and foremost an African country in which the whites constituted a minority.

The projected Black Republic was conceived as the apex of a revolutionary strugged waged by the African peasantry, through their peasant associations, the national liberation movement, and in alliance with the Communist Party, as the class organization of the working class. The first task on its agenda would be the resolution of the agrarian question, the establishment of organs of popular power, and uprooting the whole edifice of the colonial-racist state. The democratic republic would have a national form—it would be black—but a democratic content, expressed both in its social character, the peasant/worker alliance, and in the institutional guarantees of the rights of national minorities.

The Black Republic thesis was the first declaration of the demand for majority rule in our country, encapsulated in the slogan—*Afrika! Mayibuye!*—which the CPSA adopted as its own after 1928. In infused a truly revolutionary content into the internationalism of the young CPSA and created the opportunity for the Marxist tradition to enter the mainstream of the national liberation movement. Advocacy of majority rule and alliance with the national liberation movement clearly demarcated Marxism-Leninism from the reformist tendencies in South African socialism. But this was an achievement won through painful struggles of the 1920s, 1930s, and 1940s, which tested the mettle of South Africa's Communists.

The most important facet of the Black Republic thesis, however, remains its laying bare the symbiotic relationship between national oppression and capitalist exploitation. The national and class dimensions are inseparable; neither can be stressed at the expense of the other; they must be read together. This was a theoretical departure which was to have the most profound implications once it was grasped by the liberation movement.

THE FREEDOM CHARTER

The Freedom Charter, adopted by the Congress of the People in 1955, is the common programmatic statement of the liberation alliance comprising the ANC, the South African Communist Party, and the South African Congress of Trade Unions (SACTU). At the time it was drafted, it was conceived as and remains as the formulation of the strategic line of march of the South African revolution. The central features of the Freedom Charter are clearly stated in its first five clauses: the demand for majority rule, institutionally expressed as adult suffrage; the abolition of all forms of racial and national domination, to be embodied in statutory rights for all national groups; the transference of the key centers of economic power to the ownership of the people; the dismantling of the white minority's monopoly over the best agricultural land; and civil liberties for all. This is a program around which the widest spectrum of forces opposed to white racist domination can be mobilized. Within this broad alliance of class forces it is generally recognized that the vanguard contingent is the black working class. As conceived by the ANC and its allies, the line of march entails a national alliance of all the oppressed and exploited strata, under the leadership of the black working class, to dismantle the racist state and create in its stead institutions of popular power bearing the hallmark of this national alliance.

The Freedom Charter and its subsequent elaboration at the Morogoro Conference, *The Strategy and Tactics of the ANC,* [17] represent the crystallization of the theory of the South African revolution as it has evolved from these two principal sources. Though we do not claim any dramatically new theoretical contributions, there are two departures we feel we can point to.

In the Marxist tradition as we have traced it in the preceding pages, the principal controversy surrounding the relationship between the national liberation and class struggles has revolved around which of these two takes precedence over the other, or which shall be the dominant and which the derivative. Marx in his writings on India and Ireland, before 1869, seemed to be in a little doubt that the class struggle in the metropolitan countries takes precedence and would in fact result in the liberation of the colonies. His reversal of this position with regard to Ireland in 1869 had far-reaching implications both with regard to British socialism and the colonial liberation movement. If, as Marx implies, the lever must be applied in the colonies, does this not suggest that the colonial struggle can take precedence over the struggle in the metropole? The experience of the Russian revolution appeared to provide the answer in practice. But, by 1920, Lenin himself was beginning to recognize the limitations of its applicability.

South Africa presents the theoretician with an anomaly in which the metropole and the colony exist within the same national boundaries. This anomalous situation is compounded by the fact that the decisive sections of the proletariat are not of the metropole but of the colony. We can therefore suggest that South Africa will see an inversion of the Russian experience; it will be the working class of the colonized people that will take in tow the other class forces. In this context could one separate the class from the national liberation struggle? If neither takes precedence, does this then suggest that the two are coterminous? These are questions we suggest cannot be answered in the seminar room, but rather must be answered by revolutionary practice.

What then is the relationship between the Freedom Charter and the theme of our conference? We would suggest that the Freedom Charter, though itself not a socialist document or program, lays the basis for the seizure and holding of political power by the oppressed in

South Africa. The radical measures of agrarian reform and nationalization it entails will go a long way towards removing the commanding heights of the economy from the sphere of private ownership and open up the way for the socialist transformation of our country. However, the precondition for all this is the revolutionary overthrow of the Pretoria racist regime.

In conclusion we return to a point raised at the beginning of this paper, the counterrevolution directed against the efforts of southern African states to construct socialism. While we are certain that all of us have much to learn from the rich storehouse of experience already accumulated in this region, we must not minimize the grave dangers that beset us all. The primary source of all these—the one regime which is the bulwark of reaction in our midst—is the Pretoria regime. The greatest single contribution the people of South Africa, under the leadership of the ANC, will make towards socialist transformation in our region is the destruction of white domination and apartheid. We think we are justified in demanding the support of all social scientists of the region.

REFERENCES

1. *Sechaba*, July 1983, p. 7.
2. Karl Marx and Freidrich Engels, *Collected Works*, Volume 7, p. 3.
3. Karl Marx and Freidrich Engels, *Collected Works*, Volume 6, p. 552.
4. *Sechaba*, May 1982, p. 18.
5. Karl Marx and Freidrich Engels, *Collected Works*, Volume 8, p. 163.
6. *The African Manifesto.*
7. (ANC) *Programme of Action* (1949).
8. Quoted by Horace Davis, *Nationalism and Socialism*, New York 1973, p. 7.
9. Karl Marx, *The First Indian War of Independence*, Moscow 1971, p. 30.
10. *Ibid.*, p. 16.
11. *Ibid.*, p. 34.
12. *Ibid.*, p. 20.
13. *Ibid.*, p. 34.
14. Karl Marx and Freidrich Engels, *Selected Correspondence*, Moscow 1975, p. 218.
15. *South African Communists Speak*, London 1981, p. 21.
16. *Imprecor*, 1928, 68:1234–43.
17. *The Strategy and Tactics of the ANC* (Morojoro Conference).

5

Southern Africa: US Policy and the Struggle for National Independence
Ibbo Mandaza

INTRODUCTION

The prospect of black majority rule in South Africa in the near future arouses as much excitement as it does anxiety. For, as a senior member of the National Liberation Movement of South Africa said (to me) the other day, the question of South Africa's "Day of Liberation" is no longer that of *when* (it is expected in the next two or three years[1]) but *how* this outcome is to be achieved. As the theme of the Workshop—Whither South Africa?—indicates, the question of *how* is to be answered through an analysis of the historical process in South Africa. This includes, among other things, an analysis of the nature of imperialist (the US in particular) imperatives in the southern African subregion, the dynamics of the class and racial conflict within South Africa itself, and the character and course of the National Liberation Movement. This includes looking at the context of the global struggle between the US and the socialist bloc as it applies to southern Africa at this historical conjuncture. An account must be taken of both the nature of the imperialist hegemony in the region as well as the broad parameters of political and socioeconomic action that this tends to prescribe upon the struggle itself.

That the struggle in southern Africa has come this far is no mean achievement: in the late 1960s and early 1970s, even some of the African nationalists tended to share the white settler belief that black majority rule was not in the offing. However, today we stand at an important juncture at which the end of white settler colonialism in southern Africa is now on the horizon. We need to remind ourselves that such positive changes as our subregion has experienced are the cumulative result of decades of resistance on the part of the oppressed and exloited peoples of southern Africa. Yet there are some who would like us to believe that change is the result of benevolence and change of heart on the part of both the white settler colonial states and those of the international arena that had in various ways helped to sustain the systems of domination.

International opinion has changed and has brought international pressure to bear on the apartheid regime. But this is so mainly because of the impact of the struggles themselves and the realization that the end of apartheid is both immanent and imminent. Indeed there will be more violence and the need for a more coordinated approach by the National Liberation Movement is imperative if black majority rule in South Africa is to be brought closer.

In short, it is the African peoples, through the many decades of struggle, who are changing apartheid and are about to dismantle it. The history of the struggle in southern Africa as it has unfolded so far tends to contradict the theory of the "logic of protracted struggle" as one that is synonomous with total political independence and the basis for the transition to socialism.[2] The attainment of national independence in Angola, Mozambique, and Zimbabwe has not brought about the expected economic freedom nor has it brought about lasting peace, security, and genuine development for the mass of the people.

On the contrary, national independence has given birth to conditions which threaten not only the newly-won political independence but postpone the prospect of socialist construction in these societies. This is particularly true in the case of Angola and Mozambique where counterrevolutionary forces supported by South Africa and imperialism are on the rampage. There is as yet no sufficient evidence to suggest that the struggle for Namibia and South Africa will not end in a "negotiated settlement" in which imperialism and finance capital will for some time prescribe over these societies the broad parameters of constrained political and socioeconomic action.

Thus, while important gains have been made by the national liberation in the subregion, US imperialist counteroffensives remain quite real and a potential threat. Even now as we meet in this conference, there is yet another US diplomat offensive, headed by State

Department official Frank Wisner, that appears to be a step towards finding a formula for a "negotiated settlement" in both Namibia and South Africa. The precedent of the Lancaster House Agreement on Zimbabwe should alert us that there is nothing startling about this prospect. But there is danger in stretching historical parallels too far, especially in a situation such as South Africa's wherein the configuration of forces are so complex, the vested interests of imperialism so entrenched, and the forces for change so dynamic. The outcome of a "negotiated settlement" in both Namibia and South Africa might be even more unfavorable to the National Liberation Movement than appeared to be the case in the Zimbabwe situation of 1979–1980. The dynamics of the post–Lancaster House situation in Zimbabwe are sufficiently developed, at least to enable us to see the pros and cons of negotiations.[3]

What are the implications of the current internal upsurge in South Africa? What are the prospects and capacity of the African petit-bourgeois leadership to coordinate both the internal and external factors into a unified strategy vis-a-vis both the white society and imperialism? What will be the nature of the relationship between the national liberation movement and the immense social forces— including the labor movement—that have been generated in South Africa? That is, in the conditions of struggle, who will resolve the problems of the masses? The mass upsurge in South Africa has already superceded anything we have seen in either Angola, Mozambique, or Zimbabwe. In such a situation, can be ruled out the possibility of new alliances between say, international capital, the white settler factor, and the African petit-bourgeoisie that will seek to contain these social forces?

In short, what is the likelihood of a black majority-ruled South Africa constituting a challenge to imperialism—or will it reinforce the current patterns of domination, insecurity, and underdevelopment for the mass of the people? The questions are numerous and need to be considered carefully in a concrete analysis of the South African situation.

The purpose of this paper is to briefly survey US policy in response to developments in the subregion in general and South Africa in particular. The intention is not to accord imperialism "apparently all conquering power, total clarity and unanimity of purpose, and almost omnipotent causal potency," to quote Gavin Kitchin[4] in his critique of those radical African scholars that have sought to emphasize the role of imperialism in the current historical conjuncture. Nor should the analysis of the role of imperialism overlook the nature of the indigenous social forces or the expression of class and other social contradictions within the African countries themselves.

Our analysis is not oblivious to the role of the postcolonial state and the petit-bourgeoisie class that leads it. But the concept of imperialist hegemony also includes within it the nature of the dominated society, its colonial legacy, the resultant class structure, and the postcolonial state. It is not that imperialism thereby imposes a permanent solution in its favor and thereby subsumes all internal contradictions and antagonisms. On the contrary, these societies continue to be character- ized by sharp conflict, both internal and in antagonism to imperialism itself. But in seeking to bring about a political solution (stability) in its favor, imperialism tends within a particular historical conjuncture to prescribe upon the dominated society broad parameters of political and socioeconomic activity.

The analysis is presented not on the basis of some fatalistic acceptance of the inevitability of neocolonialism in southern Africa. It seeks to highlight the specter of imperialism in the context of US policy in southern Africa; but it does so also in the hope that as political analysts and activists, we will be able to develop deeper insights into the current condition and thereby develop better and more effective strategies for advancing the struggle. In brief, there appears to be no effective alternative strategy to that of seeking to achieve national unity, regional unity, and Third World internationalism on the basis of a united opposition to (imperialist) policies that seek not only to forestall socialist construction, but even to undermine national inde- pendence. The attainment of black majority rule in South Africa constitutes a fundamental break with a past characterized by insecurity for the people of southern Africa (and Africa), and lays the basis for an effective challenge to imperialism on a world scale. It is for this reason, perhaps, that others from a different perspective have concluded that the "sudden collapse of white rule in South Africa would lead to a catastrophe comparable to that of the Russian revolution itself."[5] The imperatives of US policy in southern Africa then should be obvious: the attempt to avoid such a "catastrophe."

US GLOBAL POLICY IN PERSPECTIVE

US policy in southern Africa must be understood as part and parcel of the global policy of a superpower bent on preserving the international capitalist system. In fact, V.I. Lenin's theory of "Imperialism: The Highest Stage of Capitalism"[6] is both self-explanatory and relevant today. The main features of imperialism are as follows:[7]

1. The gap in economic development between the industrial-
    ized Western (and European settled) countries and those
    restricted to primary production, a gap that is widening
    under continued imperialist domination
2. The export of capital from the more developed countries to
    the less
3. The division, especially in the late nineteenth century, of terri-
    tories throughout the world by the more developed nations
    as part of the rivalry and competition for strategic and
    economic advantages—in effect, competition for colonies—
    which led to two world wars
4. The further concentration and centralization of capital and
    the integration of the world capitalist economy into the
    structures of the giant US based multinational corporations
    or integrated monopolistic enterprises, which not only
    accelerate technological change but also control trade,
    prices, and profits
5. The decline (in the period since the Russian Revolution of
    1917) of national rivalries among the leading capitalist
    countries as an international ruling class is consolidated and
    constituted on the basis of ownership of control of the
    multinational corporations, and as the world capital market
    is internationalized by the World Bank and other agencies of
    the international ruling class
6. The evolution of global imperialist foreign policy which
    corresponds to the global interests and perspectives of the
    multinational corporations
7. The intensification of these tendencies (outlined in 4, 5, and
    6, above) arising from the threat of world socialism to the
    world capitalist system

A number of US scholars have, in recent studies, shown that the US
global policy has always been a grand and deliberate plan.

In the real world, U.S. global planning has always been sophisti-
cated and careful, as you'd expect from a major superpower with
a highly centralized and class conscious dominant social group.
Their power, in turn is rooted in their ownership and management
of the economy, as is the norm in most societies. During World
War II, American planners were well aware that the United
States was going to emerge as a World dominant power, in a

position of hegemony that had few historical parallels, and they organized and met in order to deal with this situation.[8]

This developed subsequently into the conception of "Grand Area" planning.

> The Grand Area was a region that was to be subordinated to the needs of the American economy. As one planner put it, it was to be the region that is strategically necessary for world control. The geopolitical analysis held that the Grand Area had to include at least the Western Hemisphere, the Far East, and the former British Empire, which we (the U.S.) were in the process of dismantling and taking over ourselves. . . . The Grand Area was also to include western and southern Europe and the oil producing regions of the Middle East; in fact it was to include everything, if that were possible. Detailed plans were laid for particular regions of the Grand Area and also for international institutions that were to organize and police it, essentially in the interests of this subordination to U.S. domestic needs.[9]

This is a policy based on real politik analysis of US interests; and in 1948 a Top Secret (PPS:23) document of The State Department, quoted below, made it clear that the question of human rights, justice, and economic and social progress for those dominated by the US was quite secondary in this regard.

> We need not deceive ourselves that we can afford today the luxury of altruism and world benefaction. We should cease to talk about vague and. . . . unreal objectives such as human rights, the raising of the living standards, and democratization. The day is not far off when we are going to have to deal in straight power concepts. The less we are then hampered by idealistic slogans, the better.[10]

Before becoming President of the United States, Ronald Reagan made a noteworthy statement in connection with the liberation of Angola.

> I don't know about you, but I'm concerned—scared is the proper word—about what is going on in Africa. . . . Many Americans have interpreted our interest in Africa as an extension of our own desire to achieve racial equality and elimination of injustice

based on race. I am afraid that is a naive oversimplification of what is really at issue.[11]

These views have, with varying degrees of emphasis and intensity, prompted violent and horrific US intervention in various parts of the world: Vietnam, the Caribbean, and Central America, including the overthrow of one little country—Grenada. These interventions have resulted in "huge massacre"; for example, from 1954 to 1965 the US "succeeded in killing maybe another 160,000 to 170,000 South Vietnamese, mostly peasants." From 1965 to 1975, the Vietnamese War left a death toll of "maybe in the neighbourhood of 3 million," and "perhaps a million dead" in Cambodia and Laos. Altogether five million people were killed, and "well over 10 million refugees" were created by the American bombardment and ground operations, not to mention the physical devastation of the land and other resources.[12]

The figures are much larger if one were to include those resulting from US-backed coups in such countries as Indonesia (1965) which led to the massacre of "maybe 700,000 people, mostly landless peasants;"[13] and the Philippines which, if one includes the latest episode which saw the US stage-managed replacement of Marcos by Aquino, has experienced more than 40 years of intermittent US intervention. Similarly one can turn to Africa in general and to southern Africa in particular; to the series of acts of destabilization; the accounts of CIA operations in Africa ever since the Congo Crisis of 1960 and the related assassination of Lumumba; the overthrow of Nkrumah; the well-known pattern of destabilization of frontline and SADCC states through the agency of the South African military machinery; and the support of such bandit groups as the MNR in Mozambique and UNITA in Angola.

The point can hardly be overstated: imperialism is aggressive by nature, and includes in its armory all those policies and actions designed to attain its global objectives—political blackmail, economic blockades, manipulation of "aid," and the control of the international financial institutions (the World Bank and the International Monetary Fund), in addition to open aggression, intervention, etc.

We must remember, however, that the US seeks stability in southern Africa for its own economic and strategic interests. This is particularly so in relation to what the US perceives as the threat by the Soviet Union (and socialistic bloc) to its "zones of influence" and global interests in general. In this respect, the US will of course exaggerate the "Soviet" or "Communist" threat in the context of the broad parameters of "East-West" or Cold War politics.[14] It is perhaps more correct to view the Soviet "threat" as a clumsy preemptive act of US imperialism to justify its aggressive policies. For example, in 1965, the US intervened in the Dominican Republic because of a perception that the election of Juan Bosch would lead to the creation of another Cuba. These preemptive actions have serious repercussions and further complicate the nature of superpower politics (and the threat of nuclear war). In the final analysis, Big Power politics becomes a factor in such situations as South Africa, even though it is largely acknowledged that the Soviet Union "is not a major actor in the southern African region."[15]

The amazing feature of US global policy from World War II onwards is a high degree of continuity. In fact, there appears to be no fundamental change—despite the fairly significant passage of time—in the nature and conduct of US foreign policy, from the Top Secret document, PPS:23, of 1948 (cited above) to the current "Reagan Doctrine." One writer describes the thrust of US policy under Reagan as follows:

> The Reagan Administration was moving in the direction of a strategy of confrontation with the Soviet bloc and with the socialist and radical regimes of the Third World. . . . The Administration intended to apply pressure against the Soviet Union and against those countries which it regarded as Soviet "surrogates." This pressure would be diplomatic, economic and military. This new strategy was aimed at changing the world balance in favour of the U.S. . . . so far as to suggest that it would be aimed at forcing the Soviet Union to "abandon Communism". . . . Soviet leaders would have to choose between peacefully changing their system in the direction followed by the West or going to war.[17]

In July 1981, the new US secretary of Defense, Caspar Weinberger, outlined the main objectives of "U.S. Military Strategy for the 1980's." According to Weinberger, the US "is and always should be, a global power, with global concerns and responsibilities." The task of the US government, therefore, was "to protect those interests wherever they are assailed, and, in view of our global role, we must defend and support a stable, peaceful international system." Therefore Soviet military power, which includes "the training and support of terrorists" and "the use of military assistance and proxies" was the most immediate, significant and dangerous threat to the national security of the United States."[18]

The Reagan doctrine contains two new dimensions: the need "to contain Soviet expansion" and that of "intervening in areas that the United States deemed to be part of 'The Soviet empire'."[19] The strategy was to be pursued through both conventional and unconventional means. In the period 1981–1985, covert action and special operations as well as diplomatic, political, and economic means were used "with increasingly close cooperation between the Department of Defence and the Central Intelligence Agency."[20]

Commenting on the Reagan doctrine, the magazine *Jeune Afrique* noted,

> In a bid to limit the influence of the socialist countries in Africa the present Master of the White House is trying to strengthen, if not create from scratch, reliable pro-American strongholds through the whole of the African continent. . . . [relying] on Morocco in the West, Egypt in the North, Sudan (before the overthrow of Nimieri in 1985), Somalia, and Kenya in the East, Zaire in the center, and finally, South Africa in the South."[21]

Thus by late 1983, the US was engaged in at least seven major covert operations around the world, including those against Afghanistan, Angola, Cambodia, Chad, Iran, Libya, and Nicaragua, "all of which involved the expenditure of hundreds of millions of dollars."[22] However for much of 1983 and 1984, this military strategy ("aimed at the systematic destabilization or overthrow of Third World governments") was not publicly known until the explicit outline of the "Reagan doctrine" by Mr. Reagan himself in January 1985:

> We must not break faith with those who are risking their lives— on every continent, from Afghanistan to Nicaragua—to defy Soviet-supported aggression and secure rights which have been ours from birth.[23]

In 1985, for instance, a decision was taken to openly support UNITA rebels in Angola as part of the global plan. David B. Ottaway and Patrick Tyler observe that

> Conservatives have cast the Savimbi aid issue in terms of an ultimate test of the so called "Reagan Doctrine", the administration's declared objective of aiding anti-communist "freedom fighters" in their struggles against Soviet and Cuban backed governments.[24]

THE BASES OF US POLICY IN SOUTHERN AFRICA

Within the context of the "Grand Area" global policy, it is difficult to accept the view expressed by some analysts that Africa in general and southern Africa is particular "remains less central (despite mineral wealth) than the Middle East, South Asia, and the Central American Caribbean region."[25] Equally unacceptable is the related view that because southern Africa "is not a primary concern" to US policy, "the movements of the region remain and will remain, relatively speaking, more on their own,"[26] thereby implying a degree of indifference to southern Africa on the part of the US. Recent events prove otherwise. The Reagan doctrine, as shown above, regards every part of the world (including the Soviet Union) as of major concern in terms of its imperial global interests.

As long as Africa was under the control of colonial powers, the US appeared to show a degree of "indifference" to Africa. That is, Africa's control by Europe was taken for granted until Africa began to fight back. The nature and enormity of the US reaction (and that of its allies) to revolutionary pressures in Africa in the last two decades is adequate evidence that this "indifference" was only apparent.

Many studies have documented the history of US–Africa relations in the last forty years.[27,28] More recently, the architect of current US Africa policy, Chester Crocker, summarized his country's broad objectives in Africa. Addressing a State Department Foreign Policy Conference in Washington on June 2, 1981, he stated,

> The Reagan administration recognizes that Africa is a region of growing importance to U.S. global objectives—economic, political, strategic, human and so forth. We cannot afford to neglect a region where our interests are so clearly growing and I would simply refer here in passing to the obvious facts of our long history of involvement with Africa: to the many links of culture and blood that ties an important portion of our own citizenry to Africa; to our growing import-dependence on fuel and non-fuel minerals produced in Africa, to Africa's growing place as a focus of world politics and its growing role as an actor in World politics.[29]

Accordingly, the intention is to "support regional security in Africa" and to

> cooperate with our allies and friends in Africa to deter aggression and subversion by our global adversary. We intend to assure the

U.S. and our allies fair commercial access to essential fuel and non-fuel minerals and other raw materials produced in Africa, and at the same time to promote the growing engagement of the American economy and the American private sector in Africa's growing economy.[30]

He viewed US interests in Africa as "wholly consistent and compatible with the interests of the African States themselves." Therefore, according to Crocker, the presence of Cuban troops in Africa is "inimicable to our objectives and to African interests also."[31] Implicit in the entire policy statement is the view that Africa as a whole is "rightfully" a US sphere of influence. What complicates US policy is South Africa's policy of apartheid, which has increasingly become a human rights issue in international politics with public opinion dead set against it. Until South Africa moves away from apartheid US designs are "restrained" compared to either Southeast Asia or Latin America. But as has already been pointed out, this is not to say that Africa has not had its share of the onslaught of US imperial policy nor that the future will not see emerge a pattern of action similar to that already prevalent in Latin America and Southeast Asia. Much appears to hinge on how the US perceives the South Africa developments. That is, can apartheid be abolished while keeping South Africa within the US sphere of influence?

In examining the thrust of US policy in southern Africa, it is also important to mention the relationship between the rise of imperialism and the historical phenomenon of white settler colonialism in South Africa, Zimbabwe, and Namibia. White settler colonialism can be described as a particular expression of imperialist domination or as colonialism par excellence. In the imperialist scheme of things, South Africa became and has remained the main fulcrum defining the subregion as we know it today; that is, imperialist operations in this part of the world have largely been centered there. From the fifteenth century onwards, southern Africa was recognized as constituting a vital strategic center on the route to India and the rest of the Asian and the Far Eastern subcontinents. It was *historically* inevitable, perhaps, that South Africa should feature prominently through the three successive stages of capitalist imperialism: mercantile imperialism, free trade imperialism, and modern monopoly imperialism. All these cover the modern history of southern Africa, from 1652 when the first Europeans arrived at the Cape to the present.

It is unusual to associate southern Africa with those immense material and human resources that have also been the basis of its misfortunes relative to the history of imperialism and colonization in the subregion. Numerous studies have highlighted the extent of US and Western investment in southern Africa: between 1943 and 1978, direct US investment in South Africa grew from $50 million to $2 billion (US), an increase of 4,000 percent; reached $7,200 billion (US) by 1980; and is today and annual $3,000 billion (US) in the form of profits and dividends for overseas international monopolies. In fact, Britain and American account for about 70% of the total foreign investment in South Africa; and there are now 350 US companies involved in South Africa.[32]

Similarly, there is more than ample documentation of the pattern and rate of investment in South Africa by other Western and NATO countries, notably Britain, West Germany, France, and Japan. Indeed there is a relationship between such investment and the industrial and military build up in South Africa; that is, the extent to which all this has helped to buttress the apartheid state. More recently, studies have shown the relationship between US and Western investment on the one hand, and South Africa's growing military technology and nuclear capability on the other.[33] All this has constituted the basis of South Africa's own policy of "Total Strategy" that involves, among other things,

> a militarized national security system, integrating all branches and levels of the state machinery, industry, business, the educational system and all other institutions to ensure that political control remained in white hands, more specifically in the hands of the Afrikaaner group of the ruling class.[34]

All this links up closely with the strategic role of South Africa within the overall context of US global policy. Most studies of US policy in southern Africa rely heavily on an analysis of the National Security Study Memorandum 39 (or NSSM 39) of 1969, a US policy document that outlined the Nixon-Kissinger strategy in southern Africa. The editors of a popular version of this study have dubbed it the "Kissinger Study of Southern Africa."[35] The authors emphasize that the policy is based on a careful consideration on the part of the US of its strategic and economic interests in the subregion. These interests are, in turn, related to US global interests as a whole.

The editors have summarized the "real world considerations" affecting US policy toward southern Africa as follows:[36]

1.   The strategic importance of southern Africa, particularly

with the closing of the Suez Canal following the 1967 Middle East War and the increased Soviet naval activities in the Indian Ocean

2. The US need to use overflight and landing facilities for military aircraft heading to and from Indo-China
3. Significant investment and balance-of-trade advantages to both Britain and the US in South Africa
4. South Africa's status as the major gold supplier in the capitalist world and its importance in guaranteeing the useful operation of the two-tier gold price system

On the basis of the foregoing, therefore, the objectives of US policy in southern Africa were stated as follows:

1. To improve the US standing in black Africa and internationally on the racial issue
2. To minimize the likelihood of escalation of violence in the area and risk of US involvement
3. To minimize the opportunities for the USSR and Communist China to exploit the racial issue in the region for propaganda advantage and to gain political influence with black governments and liberation movements
4. To encourage moderation of the current rigid racial and colonial policies of the white regimes
5. To protect economic, scientific and strategic interests and opportunities in the region, including the orderly marketing of South Africa's gold production

The strategic and economic resources of southern Africa have made the US a major actor in southern African affairs. From the visit of Kissinger himself to the present, US involvement surpasses even that of the former colonial master of the subregion, Britain. Thus, the 1970s witnessed the heavy hand of the US in the "detente" exercise and particularly after the Portuguese coup of 1974 that led to the success of the Liberation Movements in Angola, Mozambique, and Guinea-Bissau. Perhaps more than Britain itself, the US was quite instrumental in the Lancaster House Agreement on Zimbabwe of 1979–1980.

Option Two of the Kissinger memorandum had proposed

Broader association with both black and white states in an effort to encourage moderation in the white states, to enlist cooperation of the black states in reducing tensions and the likelihood of increasing border violence and to encourage improved relations among states in [the] area.[37]

It has also been argued by those who designed the policy that Option Two was based on the belief that "blacks cannot gain political rights through violence" and that therefore only a combination of persuading the whites into "acquiescence" and "increased economic assistance" could bring about constructive change. It has been noted that the NSSM policy document showed a "complete lack of concern over the aspirations and fate of the African people," that the US "had no genuine interest in solving racial and colonial conflicts in Southern Africa," and that in general the US became involved "not out of commitment to fundamental human rights and basic democratic principles" but "because other countries have made it so."[38]

As has already been pointed out, the content and impact of such a policy will easily put to rest the view that the US regards southern Africa and South Africa in particular as being of lesser (economic and strategic) importance than other regions of the world. In fact, such a view is invariably based on a fragmented rather than a holistic analysis of US policy in the subregion. There is even the belief that, in the words of some US official sources, "American investment in South Africa is so small," that the US has no real leverage on the South African regime in terms of desired changes towards the abandonment of apartheid; and that therefore the US can ultimately disengage from South Africa without detriment to both its regional and global interests.

This view of course is a luxury which is contradicted by recent US actions. The following analysis reveals a South African state increasingly losing the initiative, as its narrow social base is further undermined by the rising tide of international opposition to apartheid. Let me now briefly consider whether or not South Africa is indeed a "sub-imperial" power.

Ruy Mauro Marini was perhaps the first writer to use the concept of "Sub-Imperialism" in his account on "Brazilian sub-imperialism."[39] Marini defines "Sub-imperialism" as essentially "the form which dependent capitalism assumes upon reaching the stage of monopolies and finance capital."[40] But within the context of the overall imperialist strategy of trying to contain revolution and so keep the capitalist system intact, Brazilian "sub-imperialism" represents the counter-revolutionary role that Brazil plays in Latin America on behalf of the US. Viewed in the latter context, it is not surprising that the concept of "sub-imperialism" came to be applied in a similar characterization of South Africa and other clients of the US.

South Africa's economic strength in the subregion and the fact that most of the frontline and SADCC states are in fact dependent upon South Africa for trade, transport, and even employment puts South Africa in a strong position as a regional power.[41] Moreover, South Africa has the military strength and capacity to invade and occupy neighboring states in the subregion without incurring penalties. As has been explained above, sometimes South Africa's aggression is part and parcel of the US policy in the region and would tend to justify Dan Nabudere's view that "it is the US imperialists running all over, telling Vorster and Smith what to do."[42]

On the other hand, the concept of sub-imperialism might connote a relative degree of independence, on the part of the sub-imperial power, from the imperialist center, in which case the US cannot always dictate to such a force as South Africa. This poses a considerable analytical problem in the attempt to determine precisely the nature of the power relations between the US and South Africa. Indeed, the US might at times find it convenient—in terms of providing itself with a degree of latitude in its attempt to reconcile its South Africa and global policies—to view South Africa as ultimately having its own independent policies, regardless of those of the US. But this is obviously untrue, as shown by the US votes in the United Nations; invariably, the US with or without its allies always votes to frustrate concerted action by the UN.

US-South African relations are currently based on a coincidence of interests in southern Africa. That is why the US insists that the solution to the South African question must be in the context of its global design. But this observation of US-South African relations is quite distinct from that which views the US and South Africa as almost symbiotically determined to "protect apartheid together."[43] This is incorrect and reflects a gross misunderstanding of US policy in southern Africa. It arises out of a confusion of the means and goals of such a policy, the failure to realize that US policy in southern Africa is based on the pursuit of a political solution within which its economic and strategic interests remain intact and in keeping with its global design.

US POLICY, THE FRONTLINE/SADCC STATES, AND THE LIBERATION STRUGGLE

An analysis of US-South Africa relations in the Reagan era does help to highlight certain contradictions in US policy. The US has simultaneously sought to ensure a "solution" in South Africa compatible with US regional and global interests, while paying lip-service to human rights.

In its newly self-appointed role as the policeman of human rights throughout the world, the US cannot ignore the gross injustice perpetrated by apartheid. It cannot therefore be seen to openly decry human rights abuses in other parts of the world while keeping silent on the question of South Africa's denial of political rights to the great majority of its inhabitants. In fact, it was on the occasion of the 36th anniversary of the adoption of the Universal Declaration of Human Rights (on December 11, 1984) that Reagan was compelled to feel "a moral responsibility to speak out . . . to emphasize our concern and grief over the human and spiritual costs of apartheid. . . . "[44] Observers believe this statement marked a significant "turn about" in Reagan's previous position of "quiet diplomacy" on South Africa.[45]

The human rights issue becomes increasingly glaring to the US and its allies in the light of two other factors: (1) the increasing unrest and violence within South Africa itself, and (2) the consequent rising stature of the National Liberation Movement. This is a crisis that has led gradually to the collapse of South Africa's "Total Strategy" policy, both internally and externally. In fact the "Total Strategy" has not only failed, but has actually helped to mobilize blacks, within South Africa itself and in the frontline states, against the apartheid state. The Nkomati Accord and other similar attempts at "agreements" with black states are also part of this Total Strategy; but they have had the opposite effect of fueling the anger of the black masses of South Africa. It should be recalled that even the frontline states as a whole were compelled to give only a limited blessing to the Nkomati Accord. President Nyerere himself stated that "it is humiliation for African States to sign agreements in the form of Nkomati with apartheid in South Africa. . . . Africa did not want any more Nkomatis. . . . "[46]

But while the Nkomati Accords might have been a blow to the ANC[47] and all progressive forces, it has since prompted the latter into a more careful consideration of the home situation and it would appear to have given birth to new strategies and tactics. Much will depend on their ability to link within a broad strategy for national liberation the increasingly favorable home situation, the human rights movement at home and abroad, and the armed struggle. At any rate, the home situation alone is quite formidable and renders the "Nkomatis" quite ineffective as part of South Africa's strategy.

The human rights issue imposed itself on US-Africa policy. For instance, Chester Crocker in 1981 emphasized the US concern about the race issue in South Africa.[48] To some extent, this view tends to be reinforced by the conduct of the African states themselves. The basic economic, political, and military vulnerability of Africa in general, and the frontline and SADCC states in particular, has generally meant that, individually or jointly, they have had to operate within the orbit of the US policy and imperialist hegemony in southern Africa. The acceptance of the preeminent role of the US has also allowed the frontline and SADCC states substantial diplomatic and negotiating leverage with the US and its allies with respect to Africa's central objective of the decolonization of Namibia and South Africa. These states have acted as a kind of bridge between the National Liberation Movement and the US and its allies. The violence and upheavals that have accompanied the liberation struggle have had an adverse economic and military effect on them. This explains why they have been keen to negotiate for, and on behalf of, the National Liberation Movement. Their negotiating position is invariably enhanced by the rising successes of the struggle for national liberation. Sometimes this strategy of the frontline and SADCC states has meant that they have had to arm-twist the National Liberation Movement into compliance with whatever formula might be seen as the most appropriate for producing a solution that will bring about national independence.

This is in fact what happened over the Zimbabwean issue in 1979–1980.[49] It is currently happening with regard to Namibia. It will certainly happen with regard to South Africa, if and when the circumstances appear ripe enough for full-fledged negotiations. The extent to which there is usually consensus between the frontline states and the leadership of the National Liberation Movements is, of course, quite pertinent and interesting when one considers the likely developments towards black majority rule in Namibia and South Africa. Both this level of consensus and the growing stature of the National Liberation Movement of South Africa is enough basis for the possibility that soon both the South African state and the US will negotiate with the ANC.

The negotiating position of the African states has been greatly strengthened by the development of the SADCC. SADCC has developed—and continues to do so—on the basis of its strong relationship with the US and Western countries.[50] But SADCC's value is essentially in the political arena, especially in the extent to which it has mobilized the US and its allies to isolate apartheid South Africa. As had been stated elsewhere,[51] SADCC has in some respects become, for North America and Western countries who have economic links with South Africa, "a soft option, a face-saving commitment, a dubious counter-balance to their involvement in South Africa."[52] It will, however, become an increasingly harder option with the developments in South Africa itself and the subregion generally.

The last SADCC meeting in Harare, in January 1986, was a good illustration of the growing diplomatic leverage of the frontline and SADCC states in their dealings with the US and its allies on the question of Namibia, South Africa, and the subregion as a whole. The Harare SADCC meeting ended with SADCC chairman Mmusi criticizing the US for giving aid to the UNITA bandits. The meeting was a significant political and diplomatic victory for the frontline and SADCC states, enhancing the isolation of South Africa and even embarrassing US policy in southern Africa. A recent report on this meeting is an appropriate summary of this aspect of US-African relations in this period.

> Though SADCC was fully aware that it risked a serious breach with the U.S., it decided that a clear message had to be sent to Washington. SADCC Executive Secretary Simba Makoni noted that "America cannot be friends with Savimbi and friends with Angola and SADCC at the same time," a view that was greatly strengthened by the unexpectedly political tone of speeches by donor country representatives. Even before arriving in Harare, the head of the Canadian delegation . . . condemned American support for UNITA and announced an increase in Canadian aid for Angola. . . . A record 37 countries attended the Conference, and over half were represented by ministers or Secretaries of State. Eight socialist countries attended—more than before, including China and the Soviet Union. And 25 international agencies were there. . . . [53]

The Lesotho coup "actually strengthened SADCC's resolve" when the Lesotho Minister "stressed that Lesotho remained committed to SADCC, and that it will continue to pursue an independent foreign policy." Furthermore, most donor nations supported the demand for sanctions against South Africa; and the EEC signed an agreement with SADCC recognizing the latter's primacy in regional development.[54]

The liberation movements (ANC, PAC, and SWAPO) were also represented for the first time since 1980 at this January 1986 meeting. In a speech read on their behalf by SWAPO President Nujoma, the liberation movements expressed solidarity with SADCC:

> It has become imperative that we translate our common recognition that SADCC and the national liberation struggle are two sectors of a single front into action. Only by harmonising our actions can both SADCC and the Liberation Movement realize our common cherished goals.

The speech also criticized "the American, British and West German imperialist regimes" for "condoning racist oppression in Southern Africa as well as providing assistance to armed bandit gangs trying to destabilize the legitimate governments of the frontline states, notably the People's Republic of Angola.[55]

TOWARDS A NEW US POLICY IN SOUTHERN AFRICA?

This paper has sought to analyze US policy in southern Africa in terms of both its global setting and the unfolding situation in southern Africa, with particular reference to South Africa itself. With regard to South Africa in particular, the policy has for the last two decades been based on Option Two of NSSM 39 of 1969 and the belief that the African people would not attain majority rule through violence. The success of the liberation struggles in Angola, Mozambique, and Zimbabwe, of course, exposed this illusion. Yet there was no substantive change in the direction of the US policy in the subregion, reinforced as it was by the belief that the South African regime remained predominant in southern Africa. In fact, the policy of "constructive engagement" of the Reagan era is based on this assumption.

After reviewing Chester Crocker's paper, "South Africa: Strategy for Change," published in *Foreign Affairs*, Winter 1980/81, Michael Kitching and Helen Clough reached the following conclusion:

> Constructive engagement was a product of his [Crocker's] assessment that the Botha regime's secure domestic and regional position, deriving from the nation's relative economic and military self-sufficiency, limits the effectiveness of such pressures as economic sanctions or ams embargoes.[56]

The second assumption of this policy was the belief, on the basis of Prime Minister P.W. Botha's statement in 1979 that whites must "adapt or die", that South Africa was really prepared to dismantle apartheid, accept Namibian independence, and develop good relations with South Africa's neighbors. A crucial common denominator between Crocker and Botha was also the question of linkage between Namibian independence and the withdrawal of Cuban troops from Angola. It was, for obvious reasons, an issue attractive to both. But for Crocker, it has been argued, it provided the argument he needed to enlist a State Department that would otherwise have had little interest in the Namibia issue:

> By holding out the prospect of a roll back of Cuban and Soviet influence in Southern Africa, Crocker was able to get Secretary

of State Alexander Haig and the White House committed to according Namibian independence a place on the adminstration's foreign policy agenda.[57]

In turn, Crocker hoped Namibian independence thus attained "would boost US credibility throughout Africa," deal a major diplomatic blow to the Soviet Union, and "give the Botha government confidence to move faster with its internal reform program, which would in turn confirm the merits of constructive engagement."[58]

Given the changes in the balance of power in South Africa brought about by the collapse of Portuguese colonialism and the independence of Zimbabwe, the Botha regime's "Total Strategy" was bound to fail. Against the background of mass unrest in South Africa, the Botha regime could not easily give up Namibia as an important buffer zone. Nor did it have time to reform apartheid to the point where it would be acceptable to the majority of the oppressed inside South Africa itself.

In fact, by late 1984, the Namibian issue was overtaken by the South African situation itself, with the US now pushed into the position of applying pressure against South Africa. Thus, from a previous position in which South Africa was perceived as predominant in the subregion and quite stubborn, there emerged a position wherein the US tended to acknowledge that it can in effect tell South Africa what to do.

On April 16, 1985, US Secretary of State George Shultz made a policy statement that might be interpreted as representing this shift from the constructive engagement policy. There was still the recognition of South African white opinion as a "vital" key to change. But there was equally the recognition that blacks had clearly become a factor, "saying they are no longer willing to live under a system that denies them fair political participation; both demography and economics are on the side of those challenging the old order." There were, Shultz said, limits to what the US could do.

> Nevertheless, we are not without potential to affect events. While the Soviets can fan conflicts and supply the implements of war to pursue them, they cannot produce solutions. That peacemaking role can only be played by a power that has a working relationship and influence with all the parties, including, of course, South Africa.[59]

Shultz went on to list the results, so far, of this peace-making role and positive influence on South Africa which he said led to the Nkomati Accord of March 1984 and "helped Angola and South Africa agree" on a plan for the withdrawal of South African forces from Angola and control of SWAPO and Cuban troops in southern Angola. This "helped bring about" understanding between Lesotho and Botswana on the one hand, and South Africa on the other, averting potential conflict." And the policy also

> helped move Mozambique away from heavy dependence on the Soviet camp and closer to true non-alignment. We demonstrated to Mozambique that its best interests are served by closer cooperation with the West, and by rejection of confrontation with South Africa. The trend of our relations with Mozambique is positive and needs further encouragement.[60]

Shultz's policy statement constituted an important public assertion of what US aims are in southern Africa. The policy now is to move quickly to "reconcile" all antagonistic forces in the subregion in the interests of US policy, and in order to foreclose opportunities for the growth of Soviet influence. As we have already outlined above, the frontline and SADCC states themselves tend to give credence to this position. They will invariably complain about aspects of US policy—particularly with regard to South Africa—but, as a US diplomat explained to me, "No one is saying to us to get out of the region. . . . No one has told us to pack our bags and go. . . . They want the U.S. to be constructively engaged in southern Africa.

There has been much controversy about the US decision to support UNITA in Angola. But it is significant that even in the US this decision is being seen as an "aberration," a departure from this new policy that seeks to "reconcile" all forces in the subregion within a US framework that keeps out the Soviet Union and forestalls the development of Socialism in any of the states in the region. The "left wing" (which, it is said, is where Crocker now stands in relation to the "hawks") of the US State Department argues that the decision to aid UNITA is a bad one, particularly at a time when even the Angolans had shown a willingness to negotiate with the US.

> Opponents of US involvement in Angola who include 500 academic specialists on Africa who have petitioned congress to block aid to Savimbi, are warning that the United States is heading for an entangling, and inevitably damaging, alliance with South Africa that will have repercussions for American foreign policy in black Africa.[61]

CONCLUSION

As the struggle intensifies in South Africa and the Botha regime is seen to have lost control, it is possible that the US State Department will see "reason" and modify their posture in keeping with the advice of their advisers "on the ground" in southern Africa. We can expect a greater level of agreement between the US and the frontline/SADCC states, provided the US is seen to exert more and more pressure on South Africa. Those in the US calling for greater accommodation with the frontline and SADCC states will argue that neither are really "flaming communists," and that "all that the Africans want is black majority rule and the sooner they are allowed to get it, the better for Southern Africa and the US itself."

These are the bases for a "negotiated settlement" in South Africa. The possibility that the Namibia question will be resolved sooner rather than later is but one indicator that the US is now determined to put pressure on South Africa. But it could also be the first step towards an attempt to get the South African state to negotiate with the national liberation movement, seek safeguards for the whites, and impose direct and indirect constraints on the new state so as to ensure "stability."

The point often cited about the large white population having its roots in South Africa can often be exaggerated, and might even be suggestive of a racist (or inverted racist) posture that sees history from the point of view of the white factor alone. At any rate, population sizes and ratios are quite relative; and Zimbabwe is both an indicator that this could also happen in South Africa and a "model" that both the US and the Africans might be considering in terms of a future South Africa.

At any rate, there is now growing opinion, in both South Africa and the US, that only the involvement of the National Liberation Movement in any kind of "talks" will help stem the rising ride of unprecendented mass unrest.

The question is, however, whether the National Liberation Movement will be able to coordinate this storm in its future; what alliances it is likely to forge in the pursuit of state power; and what the role of the US and its allies is likely to be in such a situation, depending on how it perceives its long-term interests both regionally and globally. But these are some of the questions that this workshop will seek to answer.

NOTES

1. He thought 1990 was a bit too far; 1987 or 1988 was a more realistic forecast.
2. For a critique of the romantic rendition of the armed struggle, see Ibbo Mandaza, "Introduction," *Zimbabwe: The Political Economy of Transition, 1980–1986*, Ed. by Ibbo Mandaza, Dakar, London, Harare: CODESRIA Book Series, 1986.
3. *Ibid.*
4. "Politics, Method, and Evidence in the 'Kenyan Debate' ", *Contradictions of Accumulation in Africa: Studies in Economy and State*, Ed. by Henry Bernstein and Bonnie Campbell, 1985.
5. Michael Howard, cited by Bernard Magubane, "South Africa: 'A Luta Continua' ", Paper presented at the Sixth AAPS Bi-Annual Conference, 1985, p. 5.
6. Progress Publishers, Moscow.
7. Ibbo Mandaza, "Conflict in Southern Africa", Paper prepared for the United Nations University Project on Peace, Development and Regional Security in Africa, 1985, p. 9.
8. Noam Chomsky, "Intervention in Vietnam and Central America," *Monthly Review*, 37. 4:3.
9. *Ibid.*
10. *Ibid.*, pp. 4–5.
11. *Africa Report*, 24.4 (July-August 1980):4. *The American Enterprise Institute for Public Policy in 1978 issued a publication entitled Grand Strategy for the 1980s. One of the articles, written by General Maxwell D. Taylor, formerly US Chief of Staff and President of the Foreign Intelligence Advisory Board, spoke directly of the "growing appreciation" on the part of the United States "of the future economic importance of the resources of the region" (i.e., Africa). This, of course, had nothing to do with the concern for the interests of African people.*
12. *Ibid.*, p. 12.
13. *Ibid.*, p. 13.
14. See for example such alarmist analyses as that by Colonel Robert R. Collins (U.S. Army), "Soviet Influence in Sub-Saharan Africa," *Military Review*, 65:4 (April 1985).
15. Sean Gervasi, "The Reagan Doctrine and Southern Africa," Notes for a Paper to The Colloquium on Security and Development in Southern Africa, Paris, 1986.
16. *Time Magazine*, August 4, 1986, p. 9.
17. *Ibid.*
18. *Ibid.,*
19. *Ibid.*
20. *Ibid.*
21. *Jeune Afrique*, 1138 (October 27, 1982):33.
22. Sean Gervasi, *op. cit.*
23. *Ibid.*

134   Whither South Africa?

24. *The Guardian*, February 16, 1986.
25. William G. Martin and Immanuel Wallerstein, "Southern Africa in the World Economy, 1870–2000: Strategic Problems in World Historical Perspective," Paper for the International Colloquium on Security and Development in Southern Africa, Paris, February 24–25, 1986.
26. *Ibid.*
27. See, for example, L.A. Jinadu, *Human Rights and U.S.-African Policy Under President Carter*, Nigerian Institute of International Affairs, Monograph Series No. 5, 1980.
28. Ibbo Mandaza, "Conflict in Southern Africa," *op. cit.*
29. Official Text of the International Communication Agency, Tuesday, June 9, 1981.
30. *Ibid.*
31. *Ibid.*
32. Ibbo Mandaza, "Conflict in Southern Africa", *op. cit.*, p. 14.
33. See, for example, *"Nuclear Collaboration with South Africa,"* Report of United Nations Seminar, London, 1979.
34. M.M. Ncube, "The U.S., South Africa and Destabilization in Southern Africa," *Journal of African Marxists* (October 6, 1984):32.
35. Mohamed A. El-Khawas and Barry Cohen, Title???, Nottingham: Spokesman Books, 1975.
36. *Ibid.*, pp. 24–25.
37. *Ibid.*, p. 84.
38. *Ibid.*, p. 26.
39. *Monthly Review*, 23:9.
40. *Ibid.*, p. 15.
41. See, for example, Mohamed A. El-Khawas and Barry Cohen, *op. cit.*; Ibbo Mandaza, "Imperialism, the 'Frontline' States and the Zimbabwe Problem," UTAFITI (Journal of the Faculty of Arts and Social Sciences, University of Dar es Salaam) 5:1 (1980):129–163; Rod Bush, "Editor's Introduction: The United States and South Africa in a Period of World Crisis," *Contemporary Marxism* 6 (1983):1–13.
42. *Imperialism, the Social Sciences and the National Question* (Tanzania Publishing House: on behalf of the African Association of Political Science (AAPS), Dar es Salaam, 1977) p. 60.
43. This is the wrong conclusion drawn by M.M. Ncube, "The U.S., South Africa and Destabilization in Southern Africa" *Journal of African Marxists* 6(October 1984).
44. Cited in *The Herald*, Harare, December 12, 1984.
45. *Ibid.*
46. *The Herald*, Harare, November 24, 1984.
47. Thabo Mbeki, Member, National Executive, ANC, in a televised interview of the *Monthly Forum* of the AAPS Zimbabwe National Chapter, Harare, November 7, 1984.
48. See note 29.

49. See, for example, Ibbo Mandaza, "The Post-White Settler Colonial State in Zimbabwe," *Zimbabwe: The Political Economy of Transition*, Ed. by Ibbo Mandaza, *op. cit.*

50. See, for example, Thandika Mkandawire, "SADCC Cooperation: Problems and Prospects," Yash Tandon, "SADCC and the Preferential Trade Area (PTA): Points of Convergence and Divergence," and Ibbo Mandaza, "Some Notes and Reflections on SADCC," in *Regional Development at the International Level*, Ed. by T.M. Shaw and Yash Tandon, AAPS/CPSA publication, London, 1985.

51. Ibbo Mandaza, "Some Notes and Reflections on SADCC," *op. cit.*

52. *Ibid.*, p. 139.

53. *Africa Confidential* 27.4(February 12, 1986).

54. *Ibid.* I was also present at this SADCC meeting.

55. Consultative Conference of SADCC, Harare, January 30, 1986.

56. Helen Kitchen and Michael Clough, "The United States and South Africa: Realities and Red Herrings," *Significant Issues Series*, VI.6:3.

57. *Ibid.*, p. 4.

58. *Ibid.*, p. 5.

59. USIS Special Report, April 16, 1985.

60. *Ibid.*

61. David B. Ottaway and Patrick Tyler, "Agencies at Odds Over Savimbi's Chances," *The Guardian* (February 16, 1986).

6

On the Question of Women in South Africa*

Dr. Ivy Matsepe Casaburri

INTRODUCTION

There have been several approaches to the "woman question" even among Marxists and radical analysts. These have tended to define the parameters of the debate on the woman question. Each approach has a different focus or places analytical emphasis on different aspects of women's oppression or subordination.

Radical feminists believe that the position of women is primarily determined by a partriarchal sex system and that the division of labor by class and race stems from that system. The elimination of gender oppression, it is assumed, would also remove all other forms of oppression. Consequently, women are the most revolutionary group and they must work (if possible separately from men) to achieve sexual equality. The inadequacy of this theory for South Africa (as well

---

*The race terms used to denote social groups within the South African social formation conform to a large extent to the categories used within the social formation. However, I do not accept the racist categorization of apartheid ideology imbedded in them. They are used merely as a label denoting a social group.

137

as for other countries in the world) is rather obvious as will be shown later.

Some Marxist feminists, sticking close to the classics, see the condition of women as deriving from their class position. They use Marxist categories of the labor process, namely in production and reproduction, to define the role of women. According to such feminists the struggle of women is basically against capital in conjunction with other workers.

With the growth of the feminist movement, more subtle positions have been taken among socialist feminists, incorporating elements from both of the above. Primarily, it is now argued that there are two systems of oppression facing women—patriarchy and class. the former system oppresses all women. The latter system oppresses all.

Black feminists however criticized these approaches on the basis of their lack of consideration of the "race question." It was argued that even within the different classes black men and women were oppressed and that blacks form (in most countries) the majority of the working class, or the greater proportion of blacks are working class. Strategically, therefore, the struggle of black working class women is the essence of what all women's struggle is all about. It is argued that this struggle is one against all forms of oppression: class, race, and gender.

Though the above theoretical debates have developed mainly in the advanced Western economies, especially the United States, they may have some implications for South Africa as it is confronted by similar questions. However, we have to be careful not to impose debates or categories developed in different cultural contexts and under different historical conditions and in highly advanced economies on South Africa. The specificity of the South African social formation is para-mount in analyzing the woman question in that country.

A number of commentators have remarked unfavorably about the lack of development of a feminist movement in South Africa especially among African women who are seen as the "most exploited" of social groups in the country. Few analysts of South Africa had until fairly recently paid serious attention to the woman question. But these analysts have also differed in their approach to the question. There have been those that focus on the structure of society, specifically Wolpe's theories,[1] to explain women's position and those that have emphasized the notion of class struggle—a notable proponent being Bizzoli (1983).[2] Both approaches have been criticized however for neglecting culture as an important dimension in the analysis of women in South Africa.

The approach followed here recognizes a constant interaction between political, economic, ideological, and cultural factors as well as between structures and social actors because they are bound in a dialectical relationship. This approach allows for different levels of investigation and analysis—at the abstract level of theory as well as at the concrete level at which social agents act to make history. It allows us to analyze women as members of the dominant as well as the subordinate groups along different dimensions.

The position of women in South Africa and their experience of oppression is structurally determined by economic, political, ideological, and cultural factors. However, this is not the only determinant. Class struggle or the conscious struggle to change that position also helps to shape their oppression. While structural factors tend to dominate, we also recognize that classes, races, and other social groups may indeed act to bring about changes in those structures. This approach is true to the analytical tradition that asserts that people make history, but do not do so under the conditions of their own choosing.

It has correctly been pointed out that to understand the subordination and exploitation of women we must look to the specificity of the process of the formation of the labor force. The tendency has been to treat this as a mere function of the requirements of capital. A cautionary note must also be struck in this connection because as Tilly (1980)[3] points out, labor force formation is also a consequence of the strategy households employ in response or reaction to demands of capital.

It has often been stated that in South Africa women suffer different forms of oppression as women, as oppressed workers, as oppressed blacks, all of the above, or combinations of these forms of oppressions. African women, it is generally stated, suffer all three. The starting point of this brief analysis of the South African society aims to not only make us think through the dynamics of race, class, and gender but of culture as well. The recognition of and respect for real differences of class, race, and culture of women in South Africa enables us to deal with the different ways the different women—African, colored, Asian, and white—experience their subordination and the different implications of that subordination.[4] These are not merely academic issues but are important for political mobilization of women, especially of those groups that have previously been perceived to be marginal to the struggle for national liberation but whose importance has now been recognized.

But the specificity of South Africa's historical development and the development of racial capitalism presents us with yet another set of factors within which to contextualize this analysis. Therefore an understanding of the historical, material, and attendant ideological conditions which structure different women's positions and consciousness of their oppression is also necessary.

However these are complex issues and this paper does not intend to be an exhaustive analysis, but attempts merely to raise questions and issues that are important in determining future directions for a democratic South Africa on the question of women. We assume this question to involve "an awareness of woman's oppression and exploitation [in society, at work, and within the family] and conscious action by women and men to change this situation."[5]

My intention in this paper is not to provide all the answers to the complex question but to provoke discussion on a subject that affects such a large part of our population and which touches upon key aspects of mobilization that confront the liberation movement—a movement often accused of paying only lip-service to the oppressive conditions of women.

HISTORICAL CONSIDERATIONS

We argue that historically the oppression and exploitation of African women is in the first instance due to the economic and political interests of international capital as well as that of the white ruling class. In the second instance it is in the interest of all allies of the ruling class who benefit from the perpetuation of the socioeconomic privileges of whites and ideological and cultural subordination of all Africans by those who control the state.

While we recognize that not all African women experience their oppression in exactly the same way, a large proportion of African women have had their position structured by the integration of African economies into the world market and by such phenomena as land and agricultural policies and especially the migrant labor system. Colonial history and administrative reports are replete with concrete evidence of the visions white colonialist administrators and mining capital had of the role of African women in the political economy of South Africa—that of subsidizing the low levels of remuneration of migrant laborers and thus efficiently exploiting the labor of all Africans in those regions that supplied such migrant labor.[6] Different policies were pursued in the different areas but they were based on the same rationale. The economic rationale of the policies that had been pursued for quite some time were clearly expressed by the following extract from the South African Native Affairs Department Report, which states

> that the provision of subsistence for the family of the worker, which is left behind in the reserves, forms a vital subsidy to wages which the worker receives in those industries without which those industries (the goldmines, for instance) could not be carried on.[7]

The modes of labor control devised, the reproduction of these modes, and their ideological and cultural support systems necessitated a restructuring of African kinship, family, and cultural traditions. One of the mechanisms used to achieve this was changes in the law affecting women and marriage so well documented by H.J. Simons.[8]

Numerous changes were made in the restructuring of these African societies. Some were grafted onto aspects of culture and/or traditions which were unfavorable to women and entrenched their subordination, for example the institutionalization of the junior status of African women. A good example of this are the changes that matrilineal societies of northern Namibia have undergone. In their case much of the laws, traditions, and kinship patterns that gave women a relatively strong position have been completely eroded and replaced by patriarchal structures.

Although the subsistence base upon which African women could initially produce to augment low wages of male migrant labor has been totally eroded, the system itself has not changed. Consequently, women have had to be drawn into new forms of productive activity themselves, for example seasonal migrant labor and/or participation in informal sector activities, or else be driven to greater levels of poverty. The increased poverty level of the Bantustans is clear proof of this trend.[9]

It has been argued that capitalism is being blamed for the oppression of women when in actual fact such oppression preceded the development of capitalist relations. It cannot be denied that asymmetrical gender relations were antecedent, but other asymmetrical relations also eisted which mediated this gender asymmetry. For example, in African culture, age was an important aspect of hierarchical relations among Africans. The role of "gerontocracy" remains unexplored in the analysis of these hierarchical, asymmetrical relations across gender lines.

For example, Bizzoli has argued that it is the ability of African societies to control the labor of women that resulted in women remaining behind when the men went on migrant labor contracts. But is was the young men who were sent out initially—not all men. The ability to control the labor of young men was couched in numerous cultural traditions. Today, under totally different historical and economic conditions, women continue to be prohibited from leaving reserves or Bantustans by a myriad of legal and administrative measures that have nothing to do with African men's oppression of women, but have everything to do with racial, political domination of Africans. We should however also see the initial "youthful maleness" of migrant labor as a strategy African households employed for survival—both economic and cultural. That it was detrimental to women however cannot be denied.

In other areas of South Africa the position of African women was not structured via the migrant labor system but through the exploitation of family labor via the land tenancy system—in the Free State and Transvaal especially but also in some parts of Natal.[10] Unlike their other counterparts, these women did not experience their exploitation indirectly but very directly from very early in the process of integration into the world market economy. The effective expropriation of land and the changing structure of tenancy relations resulted, for example, in the early proletarianization of African women in the Free State as compared for example with Natal. This explains the difference in the early composition of the domestic service sector (an early step in the proletarianization of women) between two provinces—namely predominantly African female in the former and initially male-dominated in the latter.

A third group of women were those that belonged to the strata of small landed peasantry and traditional elite among the different ethnic groups. Different traditions and property relations regarding gender affected the women but generally for all these women their rights in land and property became severely circumscribed or totally eliminated. It is from this stratum that most of the early professionally trained women came. Today most of the middle class professional and commercial petty bourgeois women have their roots in this strata but some of them are women from other socially mobile families whose urban residence was able to allow them access to education, employment, and some commercial activities.[11]

Women, thus differently constituted historically, are today located in different positions in the labor structure and are affected differentially by residential laws (e.g., those allowed to live in "white" areas by Section 10 laws) and by 'citizenship' to Bantustans. Each of these conditions structure African women's consciousness of their oppression in present day South Africa.

The "Colored "population group has it historical origins in the inter-marriages of various population groups in the Cape—Africans, Khoi, Malays, of both slave and non-slave origins, and whites. Landless and greatly disadvantaged economically relative to the other groups, they entered wage labor very early in the history of capitalist development, mainly in the agricultural sector of the Cape. Their geographic distribution is pertinent to the analysis of women. Approximately 86% of the population is located in the Cape; 77% is urban, mainly concentrated in Cape Town and in towns stretching along the eastern Cape to Port Elizabeth with smaller concentrations in the Transvaal cities and Durban. The rural population among them is found mainly in the agricultural areas of the Cape province. Mostly Christian (only 6.3% Muslim) and 90% Afrikaans speaking, the women were drawn very early into domestic service and later into the early manufacturing industries.

These women's historical experience in the process of South Africa's industrialization has many similarities to those of many African women but their predominantly urban characteristics, cultural mixture, and slightly better social position in the racial hierarchy of the racist system mediates the manner in which they experience apartheid and gender oppression.

Indian women on the other hand have experienced their subordina-tion/oppression and exploitation in a very different manner. Their historical background differs; their position is mediated by not only membership in a special "racial category" that appears to be culturally exclusionary, but also by their position in the political economy of the geographic areas in which they are predominant.

Although the majority of Indians in South Africa are born there, they have roots that tie them to areas or origin in India. Their cultural, linguistic, economic, and religious origins as well as class positions and geographic distribution present us with several issues to take into consideration when dealing with the question of women. In other words, the structural position of these women in the society is further mediated by religious culture and ethnicity.

Ninety percent (90%) of Indians are descendents of indentured laborers; of these, approximately 70% are Hindu and 20% are Muslim. The latter group have their historical base in South Africa, not in indentured labor but in being what is called "Passenger Indians." These were Indians who paid their passages and were mainly traders from Western India. Because of the latter's class position, they were able to maintain contact with their country and areas of origin and thus reproduce their culture, especially at the domestic level but at the societal level as well.

The geographic distribution of these groups provides an added dimension: 91% of Indians are urban; of these, 82% to 85% are in Natal, the majority living in the Durban–Pine–Pietermaritzburg, vicinity and within a 150-kilometer radius. About 10% live in the industrial Witwatersrand–Pretoria complex.

Moslem Indians are concentrated in Durban and along the rail line from Durban to Johannesburg where they are mainly in the commercial sector. Approximately 90% of the Transvaal Indians are in the commercial sector.

Although Hindus form the largest group, they have different class backgrounds. The later arrivals among them did not come indentured. They were drawn from northern India and linguistically were Hindi and came from the higher castes. The ex-indentured among the Indians mainly entered wage employment as waiters, traders, hawkers, and initially also as domestics. Though many of them became upwardly mobile and moved up into other classes or strata, it is from this segment that the Indian working class is drawn.

Among both of these broad groups, religious–cultural practices continue to be reproduced especially at the household level but also to some extent at the societal level, though some of these practices may be on the decline. For example, arranged marriages—usually along religious and/or linguistic lines—occur and these may be important influences on the manner in which the women experience their oppression under a racial capitalist system.

Other social conditions may throw light on the condition of women. In Natal in1963, 64% of Indians lived below the poverty line; in 1970, 34% still lived in abject poverty. Approximately 20% of industrial workers in Natal were employed by Indians.[12] It is not certain how many of the workers are female. Should a large proportion be female, further issues are raised regarding how women experience their oppression. There is a need to investigate the concrete level and explore the implication of all the results.

The historical roots of white women are not uniform either. Ethnicity and class played crucial roles. The origins of white Afrikaner women were based on land, most of which was violently expropriated from Africans. Their differential class positions developed when the Afrikaners lost land and became impoverished and it was the younger women who were first sent into wage employment. This is yet a further example of survival strategies familes employed.[13] Those

Afrikaners able to hold on to land became eventually the agricultural bourgeoisie, and a significant force in the ruling class. However, to achieve this position they sought and obtained the alliance of the Afrikaner working class.[14-16] To obtain this alliance, the ideology of white supremacy became very necessary in order to divide the working class. Today, that racist ideology has a relative autonomy and is reproduced at both the household and the societal level.

Some white women, mainly of English background, arrived in the country as domestic servants.[17] But as the economy expanded and marriage opportunities became plentiful, these women quickly moved out of this employment,[18] as the changing structure of the domestic service sector illustrates.[19] Many working class white women at first augmented low wages of husbands by engaging in "productive" activities such as sewing, beadwork, cakemaking, etc with the help of domestic servants. But as job reservation ensured higher levels of remuneration for white men, many white working class women became full-time housewives; many entered the commercial and tertiary sectors, as our tables and J. Yawitch's findings[20] illustrate.

English-speaking women of the growing commercial, mining, and manufacturing bourgeoisie, from very early in the development of capitalism, held a privileged position and were later joined by the Afrikaner and immigrant women who moved into this class and other priveleged strata. The ideology of racism as well as that sexist ideology that enshrined their "pedestal" position, served the interest of these women very well. It is within their households especially that those racist, sexist, and class ideologies that oppressed African women were reproduced on a daily basis as well as generationally (in the rearing of white children). Of course these ideologies were reproduced at the social level through the massive ideological apparatus of the state, via schools, the media, and the church.

WOMEN'S PARTICIPATION IN THE ECONOMY

Agriculture and Service Sectors

Women's position in the structure of the economy, as has been shown in numerous studies, has implications for them. The participation of African women in the economy reveals several characteristics. The largest proportion (+37%) are employed in the service sector, constituting between 60% and 79% of the total labor force in that sector and about 90% of Africans in that sector. The next largest proportion of women were engaged in agriculture. Although women's incorporation took place in large numbers from the mid-1940s, the structure has not remained static as Tables I and II indicate.

Table I indicates the concentration of African women in particular sectors over time. The concentration of African women in domestic service and agriculture presents them with several problems. The domestic service sector, which employs mainly women (see Table II), isolates the individual worker, intensifies their vulnerability vis-a-vis their employers, and makes exploitation absolute. It is only in recent years that attempts have been made to organize this sector, but the very emergence of different organizations such as the Dometic Workers' and Employers' Project (DWEP), the South African Domestic Workers' Association (SADWA), and the Domestic Workers' Association (DWA) illustrates the difficulties involved. The conditions that confront these workers and the manner in which they experience their oppression were documented by J. Cock in 1980.[21] But by 1982 it became evident that this is a shrinking employment sector—partly due to the effects of recession.[22] African women's employment in the rest of the service sector increased significantly between 1973 and 1981. This was because white women moved out of some of the employment sectors such as sales, commercial clerks, etc.; "colored" and Asian women moved out of service areas such as drycleaning, shop assistants, etc., and they were replaced by African women.

Although African women increasingly entered farm wage labor in their own right, they did so mainly as irregular or casual agricultural workers. But this sector too has been shrinking due to increased mechanization of previously labor-intensive activities.[23]

The process of Africanization and feminization of these sectors of the economy was not accidental but was a result of a conscious search for the cheapest labor as well as a result of household survival needs that demanded more and more wage earners. The labor laws that had excluded these two main sectors of African women's activity from legal organization and bargaining, protective legislation, workmen's compensation, etc., reinforced women's vulnerability and powerlessness. This in turn increased the dependence of women on males—kin as well as non-kin. The residential and citizenship measures that control their movement[24] exacerbate these women's vulnerability, powerlessness, and dependence—which all help to shape their consciousness/awareness of the oppression and exploitation.

Domestic service and farm labor are also employing significant numbers of "colored" women in the Cape. Table II indicates their proportion in selected urban areas in the domestic service sector. In Cape Town in 1970 they constituted almost 70%; that same year they formed between 10.2% and 11.2% of this total sector in the country.

TABLE I. ECONOMICALLY ACTIVE AFRICAN FEMALES BY OCCUPATIONAL CATEGORY.

Occupation	1921 Number	%	1936 Number	%	1946 Number	%	1960 Number	%	1970 Number	%
Professional/Tech.	2,312	0.1	4,261	0.2	10,135	0.9	25,487	3.0	55,431	2.7
Administrative	—	—	10	—	21	—	258	—	40	—
Clerical	44	—	16	—	100	—	1,000	0.1	5,379	0.3
Sales	425	—	226	—	567	—	3,372	0.4	17,661	0.9
Service	163,009	10.2	243,852	12.7	445,401	37.7	495,167	59.1	730,345	36.8
Agricultural	1,412,289	88.4	1,659,350	86.5	667,618	56.6	192,560	23.0	871,968	43.9
Mines	531	—	—	—	—	—	12	—	1,399	0.1
Transport/Com- munication	3,234	0.2	146	—	385	—	424	0.1	3,024	0.2
Production	12,191	0.8	3,373	0.2	8,345	0.7	22,296	2.7	82,556	4.2
Unclassifiable	2,942	0.2	8,085	0.4	47,607	4.0	97,713	11.7	218,144	11.0
Total	1,596,977	100.0	1,919,319	100.0	1,180,179	100.0	838,289	100.0	1,985,947	100.0

Source: South African Department of Statistics, Population Census Report No. 02–05–04.

TABLE II. PERCENTAGE DISTRIBUTION OF DOMESTIC SERVANTS BY RACE
AND SEX IN ELEVEN PRINCIPAL URBAN AREAS IN SOUTH
AFRICA.

Urban Area	African		White		Colored		Asian	
	F	M	F	M	F	M	F	M
Cape Town	20.3	4.2	—	—	68.5	4.2	—	—
Port Elizabeth	72.8	5.3	—	—	20.9	0.8	—	—
East London	89.0	8.3	—	—	2.5	0.3	—	—
Kimberley	70.4	12.4	—	—	14.9	2.3	—	—
Natal								
Pietermaritzburg	65.8	33.0	—	—	0.3	0.3	—	—
Durban	59.5	38.8	—	—	0.7	0.1	—	—
Transvaal								
Pretoria	77.1	20.3	—	—	2.3	0.3	—	—
Witwatersrand	75.9	22.6	0.1	0.1	—	—	—	—
Free State								
Bloemfontein	80.8	14.8	—	—	3.7	0.7	—	—
Vaal Triangle	84.3	13.5	—	—	2.2	—	—	—
OFS Goldfields	85.6	11.7	—	—	1.8	0.9	—	—

Source: South African Department of Statistics.

Because these women have "urban rights," they do not suffer the residential insecurities of African women. The racial attitudes of employers are perhaps less discriminatory. But conditions of service were found to be extremely poor and wages extremely low, and in some cases lower than those of African women (UCT Wages and Economics Commission, 1973). The same structures of domination/subordination and racial, class, and sexist ideologies that affect African women also affect them. But employers and/or the system have often used measures to divide the two groups. The employers may use the dichotomies of rural (illegal)/urban, African/colored, in their deliberate choices of domestic workers as a strategy to divide and rule and hence control these workers at the individual level—a tactic that is especially helpful to the dominant classes. The difficulties experienced in organizing these domestic workers nationally (besides those that derive from the isolated conditions of services) are partly due to all the above factors.

"Coloured" women's employment in the farming sector increased as their men moved out of this sector. Their conditions of service have been some of the most abhorrent. Besides extreme exploitation, they have been subjected to gross sexual harrassment by employers.

Although it is illegal to use the old "tot" system of payment, these women continue to be paid in this manner. Consequently there has been a tremendous increase in the rate of alcoholism among women in this sector.

Industrial Production Sector

A sector that employs large numbers of women is the manufacturing industry. The changing racial composition of the female labor force is a result of several factors, among which are a changing structure of the economy and racial and sexist ideologies regarding female labor. The major employers of women are the apparel, textile, food, leather, and electronics industries.

As Table III shows, female employment in manufacturing remained constant at 15–16% between 1946 and 1960. By 1970 it had increased to 19% and by 1976 to 21%. Clearly evident however is the decline in the proportion of white females and the relative constancy of colored females. This sector has been and continues to be a major source of wage labor for colored women. The decline in white females was compensated for by the increase of African and Asian women. This pattern is indicative of the following facts:

A. These small sectors are labor intensive and are in constant search of ever cheaper labor, especially the clothing, food, textile, and electronics sectors.

B. Some of these industries relocated to the border area and hence increased employment of African women (whose labor is even "cheaper").

TABLE III. % FEMALE WAGE EMPLOYEES IN MANUFACTURING.

Year	1946		1951		1960		1970		1976	
Population Group	%	%*	%	%*	%	%*	%	%*	%	%*
Asian	1	(0)	2	(0)	3	(1)	7	(1)	10	(2)
African	5	(1)	8	(1)	17	(2)	29	(6)	36	(8)
Colored	36	(1)	39	(6)	40	(6)	39	(5)	34	(4)
White	58	(9)	51	(8)	40	(6)	25	(5)	20	(4)
Total	100	16	100	15	100	15	100	19	100	21

*Figures in parentheses indicate female employement as a % of total manufacturing.

C. The proletarianization of Indian women (who had hitherto not worked outside the home in any significant numbers) is a result of increasing levels of poverty in the group as well as the increasing participation of the Indian petit bourgeoisie in manufacturing.

The clothing industry is the only industry in which women make up the majority of the work force. The feminization of this sector is closely related to the low wages paid, but it is often rationalized by sexist ideologies that refer to women's "nimble fingers" and "working for pocket money." Both rationalizations have no base in reality. All these women work because they have to, especially African women.

Though these workers' conditions of service, wages, and their organization in the labor process are much better than those of their counterparts in the domestic service and agricultural sectors, they face numerous problems. The general working conditions are poor, pay is low, health conditions are at best poor. Though the social nature of the labor activity may facilitate organization, they are confronted with such problems as:

1. Trade unions are illegal in Bantustans (border areas).

2. Employers use discriminatory measures in the employment of different racial groups.

3. Employers pit men against women; for example, in cases where trade unions have pushed for equal pay for men and women, women have been dismissed.[25]

Moreover, women's participation in trade union activity has been curtailed by the household activities women must perform in daily and generational reproduction (social as well as biological) of the family. This gender subordination at the household level presents serious constraints for the necessary participation of women in class struggle as well as in the struggle for national liberation.

Professional and Petit Bourgeois Strata
The position of women within this strata in each racial category is illustrated at different historical points by Tables IV and V.

African men and women in the professional category are located mainly in three areas: teaching, medicine, and religion. Women outnumber men in the former two. Salaries, conditions of service, and taxation are biased in favor of men but the differentials are relatively

TABLE IV. OCCUPATIONAL CENSUS.

	White		African		Coloured		Asian	
	M	F	M	F	M	F	M	F
Managers & Proprietors	18,561	1,509	818	16	380	71	5,889	166
Bookkeepers	4,764	3,062	6	1	26	18	196	3
Clerks	36,040	11,183	1,756	1	310	40	1,094	15
Typists	71	14,497	8	15	1	15	4	1
Shop Assistants	14,932	15,427	1,950	126	1,067	251	5,232	181
Hawkers	992	33	1,636	83	2,065	172	3,137	339

Based on: Occupational Census 1936, in U.G. November 12, 1942.

152   Whither South Africa?

TABLE V. SOUTH AFRICAN FEMALE NURSES BY RACIAL CATEGORY 1946-1970.

	1946		1960		1970	
Racial Category	No.	%	No.	%	No.	%
African	3,013	19.1	12,789	35.5	24,677	43.9
White	12,086	76.5	20,249	56.2	25,075	44.6
Coloured	626	4.0	2,660	7.4	5,569	9.9
Indian	73	0.5	351	1.0	887	1.6

narow. The differentials along racial lines are very significant, echoing the arguments by black feminists as explained before. Among Asians, significant gender differences in participation in professional and in the commercial petit bourgeois sectors may reflect class position as well as religious culture that may constrain women's work outside the home and/or the intensity of their subordination at the household level. There is need for investigation of this.

Although women of all racial categories are located predominately within certain sectors, the changing composition of these gender-specific sectors along racial lines are also telling, as Table V shows.

As the proportion of white nurses drastically declined, that of African nurses significantly increased, while that of the other groups rose steadily. While we are not certain why this was the case, it is possible that the increasing privatization of health services may be a plausible explanation. The conditions of work are not the most pleasant and salaries are not attractive for some members of those groups higher on the racial hierarchy.

But one crucial variable in the employment in these gender–specific sector is that government is the main employer. The implications of this for all black women are obvious As government employees are prohibited from engaging in labor and political organizations and can more easily be victimized by a repressive government bureaucracy, this can severely constrain women. Their vulnerability and power-lessness is real. But under the right political conditions these women may indeed be a force that helps to undermine the regime, as the Baragwanath nurses' strike or the positions taken by many teachers during the school boycotts in 1985 seem to suggest.

WOMEN'S STRUGGLES

The preceding discussion focused on historically tracing different women's positions and the structural determinants of their oppression. However, the struggles of women have also helped to shape their experiences. Women have often acted on their own behalf, separately as well as in conjunction with men. These struggles indicate the different ways women view the intensity of their oppression.

The early struggles of women against the pass laws (1913), resulted in a more than thirty-year delay in control of their labor via this system. The revolts of rural women against the culling of cattle in Natal, against the carrying of passes in the Anti-Pass campaign of the 1950s, in the Potato and Bus boycotts, and in the Defiance Campaign are indicative of issues around which women seem to organize. These issues affected the daily lives of women and their families. Women's participation in the broader issues was smaller, partly due to the dominant ideologies defining politics as a male arena. But there is need to concretely analyze the nature and extent of women's participation in resistance against the background described earlier.

Victories won in these struggles have not improved the position of women per se, as these were later eroded by new and more repressive measures. However we may assume that the historical precedents of women's struggles have an effect on later struggles.. There is need to investigate at the concrete level if there are correlations between areas of intense political resistance by women and by men in the earlier period and those of widespread women's involvement today.

The participation of women in the broader liberation struggle has definitely increased since 1970. But even as women's participation increases, and even as consciousness of women's strategic interests rises, the main focus of attention continues to be the struggle for national liberation.

Several factors contribute to this, among them:

A. Mass removals that affected more than 3½ million people of all races between 1960 and 1982 and which have disrupted the lives of men and women in an unprecedented fashion (e.g., the Surplus Peoples Project).

B. Bantustan policies and the crystallization of class interests as well as increasing inpoverization in these areas which necessitated the forging of a united domestic/household strategy to meet the onslaught on household and community survival (despite household conflict).

C. The decline of real income for all households and the recent inflation has threatened survival, for example, in the clothing industry in 1984, earnings were 22% less in real terms than in 1948.

D. Increased unemployment among all the groups is another factor. Employment in the clothing sector went down by a high of 7.5% for Africans and a low of 0.6% for Colored.

These deteriorating economic conditions have had serious implications at the household level. The various administrative measures that make women dependent on men—for example, access to urban residency, housing, credit, land, etc., all of which are crucial to women—have exacerbated that dependence, and hence the intensity of asymmetrical gender relations at the household level. This is reflected an increase in abuse of women among all races (to which increased alcoholism is a contributory factor), the appropriation of women's property via reimposed inheritance laws that do not favor women, etc.

Women's Oppression Within the Household

The oppression of women within the household is not homogeneous. There are wide variations within and across class, race, and ethnic group depending on geographic residence, religion, and the like. The intensity with which women experience their oppression at this level is affected by various factors, such as the extent to which:

(a) the sexual division of labor within the household[26] has often laid undue burden on women for the reproduction and maintenance of the household on a daily basis as well as generationally;

(b) cultural traditions and oppressive gender ideologies that support and enforce women's oppression and exploitation are reproduced at the household level (the intensity of this oppression might be greater if these traditions and ideologies had their bases under different social and production relations and were inconsistent with the new relations);

(c) women's access (both at the level of society and of the household) to those aspects of life that may help to improve their quality of life and their power is denied or circumscribed; (productive base, knowledge, education, health, or income); and

(d) women have the ability to make or participate in decisions about themselves and their families in essential matters.

There has as yet been no thorough investigation made of how these different groups of women experience gender oppression within the household. Sweeping statements and generalizations prevail but there is need to investigate the exact nature and extent of female subordination and/or exploitation at the household level. For example, the role that dowry payment or "lobola" may play in the subordination of women may vary greatly according to whether the women are urban or rural. Pronouncements on women's subordination in the household have often reflected class and cultural biases. It is often assumed that, for example, African women or poor women are more oppressed at the household level. We cannot make such assumptions. We need to establish these by investigation. This is necessary so that we avoid imposing on the poor, the weaker, and the marginalized women new forms of oppressions. This investigation is necessary to assist in restructuring gender relations within the society and within the household for all groups of women.

Soweto and Its Aftermath

The Soweto uprising touched all classes and social groupings. It transformed people's general perceptions of the different groups, crystallizing more clearly where alliances should be forged. Students among the oppressed groups built bridges across the racist population categories. Women, in fulfillment of their reproductive responsibility, became heavily involved in protection of their children. What may be a weakness was translated into "relative strength" as women sought alliances and support, material as well as emotional, across class and ethnicity as well as race.

As political resistance against the regime intensified, the identification of apartheid as a source of women's oppression and therefore focus of attack, also intensified. Because petit bourgeois and some professional women have become beneficiaries of some of the ensuing mass struggles, women's gender subordination has become even more obfuscated. The high visibility of some women leaders in the political arena, notably women like Albertina Sisulu and Winnie Mandela and the late Victoria Mxenge, has not made matters easier.

When the UDF was formed in 1983, that broad affiliation included numerous women's organizations. These organizations reflect the responses of women to the manner in which they experienced their position and oppression. While many organizations were started to improve their conditions of life/survival, many others were started to meet the various class, professional, ethnic, and cultural needs of the various women. Trade union organizations increased female membership and appear to be paying more attention to the issues affecting women. As the UDF became more of a vehicle for forging alliances across class, race, culture, and ethnicity nationally, and the African National Congress (ANC) and its Freedom Charter became more generally acceptable to the masses of the people, the reactionary opposition to these developments has not however lacked its share of women supporters.

A case in point is the growth of the Inkatha Women's Brigade. While Inkatha Women's membership is unclear (due to the extreme pressure put on workers and professional Zulu women to take out party cards), the active involvement of Brigade members in violent acts against nonmembers reflects class and ethnic contradictions.

As these contradictions develop and mature, and fractions and strata become more defined, the lack of homogeneity among women within race is likely to surface more clearly. But possibilities for building enduring alliances in support of or in defense of "people's" interests among women are likely to increase. Whether these can be translated to serve women's strategic gender interests, however, is another matter.

Summary and Conclusions

This paper has attempted to show that women's position, their oppression, and their exploitation is not only historically specific but is specific also in terms of class, race, culture, and ethnicity. Therefore in dealing with the question of women, an assumption of homogeneity especially within racial categories is fallacious. We must acknowledge differences that derive from the multi-causal nature and extreme variability of existence across class, race, nationality, etc..[27]

This paper has also attempted to show that structural factors have been the main determinants of women's oppression but that women indeed struggle against that oppression. It speaks directly to some of the issues raised by Makamure about parallel "struggles of women workers, peasants . . . and middle class women"[28] and the ambivalence toward the struggle for women's emancipation by women themselves in Zimbabwe. It also raises important implications for Namibia where there has also been differential incorporation of women into the market economy as well as differential experience of the prosecution of the national liberation struggle.

What these suggest is that under racial hegemony, where capitalist social and production relations dominate, and where women's position within the family and in society is weak and/or insecure, the struggle for women's emancipation tends to assume a secondary role.

This raises specific questions about the role of liberation movements in restructuring asymmetrical and exploitative relations in general and women's oppression in particular. National liberation movements by their very nature of course draw upon a broad spectrum of the masses. The ANC is multi-class, race, ethnic, and culture. It does and must draw upon the broad interests and struggles of the majority of people even if it does not initiate them. But it would be safe to presume that struggle around the woman question, as defined here, should be a necessary constituent of the prosecution of the struggle for national liberation. The very mechanisms by which racial capitalism and white hegemonic classes have achieved national domination demands that this be a necessary focus if true national liberation is to become a reality.

The experiences of some societies indicate that such development is not automatic, nor is it easy. It is instructive to compare differences between revolutionary societies such as Cuba and Nicaragua. In the former, Fidel Castro in 1959 remarked about racial discrimination and "silence" about sexual discrimination. But it was not until the 1970s that the Cuban government took specific measures to address gender inequality. In Nicaragua on the other hand, it was only weeks after the Sandinista victory that the government addressed the question of sexual exploitation in the media and female representation in the army cadre and at different levels of the party in the regions and in the Sandinista leadership.[29]

Today it is no longer "taboo" to talk about the subordination of women, but it is not opportune either. It is imperative that men and women within the liberation movements—ANC and SWAPO—talk about it and spearhead that struggle. It is in particular the women in these movements, as well as those less insecure and less powerless outside of them, who must "take the knife by the sharp edge" in the fight for the liberation of women.

There will be need for the consolidation and defence of newly-won freedoms. Those forces that oppose the restructuring of the new societies will waste no time in seeking out and utilizing weaknesses. Fears and insecurity can be preyed upon and manipulated. Those of women are no exception, and the left in Chile so painfully learned when Allende was overthrown.

158   Whither South Africa?

NOTES

1. Wolpe, H. "Capitalism and Cheap Labor Power in South Africa." *Economy and Society* 1 (1972).
2. Bizzoli, L. "Marxism, Feminism, and Southern African Studies," *Journal of Southern African Studies* 4 (1983).
3. Tilly, L.A. and Scott, J.W. *Women, Work and Family*. New York: Holt, Rinehart & Winston, 1978.
4. This is not intended to emphasize differences and/or cleavages between groups but to assess the commonalities as well as the differences in order to understand and work in future cooperation.
5. Reddock, Rhonda (ed.) *National Liberation and Women's Liberation*. The Hague: Institute of Social Studies, 1984.
6. Native Economic Reports 1903 to 1948.
7. South African Native Affairs Department Report, 1931, p. 13.
8. Simons, H.J. *African Women: Their Legal Status in South Africa*. Evanston: Northwestern University Press, 1968.
9. Yawitch, Joanne. "Tightening the Noose: African Women and Influx Control in South Africa 1950–1980." Carnegie Conference Paper 82 (April 1984).
10. For a more detailed analysis, see W. Bernart, *The Political Economy of Pondoland 1860–1930*, Cambridge University Press, 1982; C. Bundy, *The Rise and Fall of the South African Peasantry*, London: Heinemann, 1979; T. Keegan, *Peasants, Capitalists and Farm Labour: Class Formation in the Orange River Colony 1902–1910*.
11. For a discussion of the African Petit Bourgeoisie, see Z. Pallo Jordan, "The African Petty Bourgeoisie: A case study of NAFOC 1964-1984," ANC Occasional Research Paper, May 1984.
12. This clearly raises questions of class tensions within the Indian population that may need investigation, especially as to whether ethnicity does or does not mitigate these tensions.
13. This speaks directly to some of the issues raised by Bizzoli.
14. Morris, M.L., 1982. . . .
15. Legassick 1977. . . .
16. Legassick, M. "Legislation, Ideology and Economy in Post 1948 South Africa," in *South African Capitalism and Black Political Opposition*, Ed. by M.J. Murray. Cambridge, MA: Scheukman Publishing Co., 1982.
17. Gaistkell, D. "Christina Compounds For Girls': Church Hostels for African Women in Johannesburg," *Journal of South African Studies* 6:1 (October 1979).
18. The tensions that existed in this sector employment of time—predominantly black male and white female—and the ideological battles it raised are very well described by the historiographer Charles Van Qnselen in his works on the Witwatersrand and explain, in part, the shift out of this sector by white women.

19. Gaitskell, *op. cit.*
20. Yawitch, Joanne. "Women in Wage Labor." *South African Labour Bulletin* 9:3 (December 1983).
21. Cock, J. *Maids and Madams: A Study in the Politics of Exploitation,* Johannesburg: Raven Press, 1980.
22. Yawitch, *op. cit.*
23. De Klerk, Mike. "Maize Farm Employment," *South African Labour Bulletin* 9:2 (November 1983):19-46.
24. Yawtich, "Tightening the Noose" *op. cit.*
25. Bird, Adrienne, "Organizing Women Workers," *South African Labour Bulletin* 10:8 (July-August 1985):76-91.
26. This aspect is often seized upon (especially by males) to trivialize the struggle of women. More and more work is being done in this regard by African women researchers and the United Nations. Comparative work with Latin American and Asian scholars is beginning to reveal the importance of the analysis and the necessity for a serious consideration of this aspect for policy.
27. Molyneaux 1985....
28. Makamure, N. "The Women's Movement in Zimbabwe," *Journal of African Marxists* 6 (October 1984):74-86.
29. Cole, Jo B. "Women's Collective Actions in Cuba: Struggles that Continue," Paper presented at Wenner-Gren Foundation Symposium No. 99, Mijas, Spain, November 1985.

7

The South African State and Africa

Sam C. Nolutshungu

South Africa has always attached considerable importance to the rest of Africa for both economic and strategic reasons. The Union inherited from British imperialism an economic sphere of influence in southern Africa characterized by the radial articulation of different colonial territories to the South African economy, and in large measure the mediation of their relations with international capital through and via South Africa which became "a centre in the periphery" with its own sub-imperial ambitions.

All the other territories in southern Africa became and were kept dependent on South Africa in a hierarchy of imperialist interests in the subcontinent which necessitated differential possibilities for economic growth and development. They became, in a way that was in principle no different from that of the Bantustans, the necessary backwaters to South Africa's industrial development, a pattern moderated only by the existence of different political centers, for example, the Portuguese imperial power and the presence of significant settler populations in Zimbabwe and Angola which gave these territories a relatively privileged status in relation to international capital. Furthermore, the tensions between South African capital and, in various ways, the British state and British capital restrained the expansion and consolidation of South African economic domination, while South Africa's own subordinate role in international capitalism, together with the necessary, self-imposed restraints on the development of its own capitalist economy, significantly hampered its outward expansion.

Nevertheless, every government since 1910 has been fully aware of the potential of intensified South African economic domination and has understood the future of accumulation in the Union (later, Republic) to be linked with expansion into the African "hinterland."

At the strategic level—military and political—the importance of the continent for white rule in South Africa has also been understood and stressed. In the first and most important instance, the imperialist order in Africa created the strategic context (the absence of significant military threats) necessary for the consolidation of the South African state on the basis of a colonial racial order. Successive South African governments feared both the arming of blacks in the rest of Africa and the entry of new powers into the politics of the continent. In the post–Second World War period this made possible the assimilation of a policy favoring continued colonial rule to a virulent anticommunism which conveniently managed to conflate the class enemies at home and the threats to the strategic order in Africa.

Ideologically, Africa has also had a central place in the evolution of the racist state in some ways comparable to "the frontier" idea in other colonial histories. But in an immediate sense, the condition of blacks in other African countries, the balance of power between imperialism and popular forces, and *a fortiori* the balance of class forces in colonial and neocolonial Africa affected in very evident ways the balance of confidence between the white power bloc and its domestic challengers. Thus in the build-up to decolonization black struggles intensified, provoking both an intensification of internal repression and an aggressive African policy. Every wave of decolonization in the rest of Africa has seen larger and more intense mass struggles accompanied by increasingly aggressive and violent state responses to both the domestic challenge and to African states.

South Africa's response to African developments has consistently been linked to its relationship with the imperialist powers in two ways. First, as already indicated, South Africa enjoyed the protection of imperialism while benefiting from the role of subordinate partner in economic terms, at least in southern Africa. Thus imperialism would open doors for Pretoria in Africa. Secondly, influence in Africa would secure South Africa's privileged status in the imperialist order both economically and strategically. So important is this relationship that however great may have been, at times, the contradictions between particular coalitions within the South African power bloc and imperialism, the state has consistently managed to contain the conflict and to reaffirm the tacit alliance with the West in Africa.

If African decolonization—particularly the decolonization of what had come to be known as the "white redoubt" in the late 1960s—presented a crisis for South Africa, that crisis was a total one, relevant at all levels of state action, domestic and international. The internal struggles in South Africa itself, as well as the conflicts between Pretoria and its African neighbors, must be seen in the context of South African resistances and adaptations to the changing capacities and strategies of Western powers and capital on which its survival ultimately depends.

The terminal phase of colonialism corresponds approximately to the period between Rhodesian UDI (Unilateral Declaration of Independence) and Zimbabwean Independence which was critical for the evolution of South African strategies, conditioning to a considerable degree state responses in the contemporary period in which Western power has to be maintained in recycled forms without empire.

DOMESTIC POLITICS

In the UDI period apartheid enjoyed, for some eight years, a position of considerable strength at home due two to main factors: it had successfully disrupted and repressed the political organization of the nationalist movement and the working class, and the liberation movements having no easy access to South African territory, thanks to the system of buffer states provided by Rhodesia and the Portuguese, could only wage a war of very low intensity. In addition, the South African economy continued to boom, benefiting in its external trade also from the sanctions imposed on Rhodesia. Despite rumblings of discontent and splits, the ruling party enjoyed the support of its strongest and potentially most troublesome provincial constituency in the Transvaal from which both Verwoerd and Vorster had emerged. The white population was on the whole contented or compliant and the blacks subdued. The state machinery and the party leadership at the highest levels were under firm, unitary control by the prime minister, aided in a decisive way by the secret police.

Repression and an economic boom stimulated investors' confidence while the difficulties arising for Britain and Portugal in southern Africa encouraged a positive valuation of South Africa by Western states both as an economic partner and as an ally in the management of the region. The succession of coups and civil wars in many of the former colonies to the North, as well as the ease with which neocolonialism had been entrenched after independence, dissipated the threat which the emergence of independent black states had been thought to portend while creating opportunities for the assertion of South African influence on the continent. South African policy in Africa and towards the world generally had an important impact on the internal functioning of the state and its legitimation in ways that would affect subsequent policies and strategies towards Africa.

In the first place, the "outward-looking policy" enabled one faction within the Afrikaner nationalist leadership to consolidate and project its power through the person of Vorster, who in his turn gained for reasons of external as well as internal politics increasing control of key bureaucratic structures. Through and with the Bureau of State Security led by a personal friend of long-standing, and the Department of Information headed by personal political allies, the Vorster faction was able to become autonomous from traditional party controls while at the same time displacing the factional conflicts to the domain of state institutions and apparatuses directly.[1] Secondly, the external campaign provided a basis of collaboration among elements of the power bloc otherwise at odds with each other over various aspects of domestic policy. Foreign policy being closely identified with the internal struggle for continued racist supremacy, the new dispositions became a rallying point for the "White Unity" now felt to be urgent as well as a pretext for the movement of the party leadership towards the accommodation of class elements—foreign and English-speaking business interests—generally still viewed with suspicion by the party rank and file, still predominantly petit-bourgeoisie and working class. Equally important, the non-Afrikaans bourgeoisie could be drawn into close collaboration with the state in the crucial areas of internal security, defense, and foreign policy, and harnessed to its defense.

Since this period also saw the expansion of Afrikaner monopoly capital and its interpenetration with non-Afrikaans capital, the approach of the state to capital corresponded to the changing class character of Afrikaner rule and the widening class difference between the top and the bottom of the party.[2] In one sense, Vorster and Verwoerd were doing nothing new, representing just another chapter in the continual adjustment of the relationship between Afrikaner capitalists and would-be capitalists through the state with big (and multinational) capital. If capital's doubts about the ultimate soundness of apartheid persisted and if, moreover, it continued to complain of the racist restriction of labor supplies and markets and, indeed, investment opportunities, the project of external expansion linked to massive state expenditure and investment linked to security and defense as well as

The South African State and Africa   165

bureaucratic empire-building could win peace—for so long as the economy continued to boom. Under Verwoerd and Vorster the state would be the unquestionable senior partner in this alliance, just as in foreign policy the institutions that they (and their personal allies) controlled would dominate. Thus, for example, the burden of supporting the Rhodesians and of manning the borders fell on the police, as did espionage and subversion. Many of the functions of the foreign service were taken over by the Information Department.

The National Party being, like all ethno-nationalist parties, inherently fissiparous, divided by class and by locality and by the political machines-within-machines which such parties invariable foster; each leader in power has minded, consolidated, created, or sought to create an organized base of his own. Vorster's functioned well until its failures undermined its authority and emboldened others to challenge it for the leadership of state and party. The collapse of the Portuguese stand in Africa, the impact of the oil price increases of the 1970s coupled with violent fluctuations in the price of gold, black revolt, and the failure of South African intervention in Angola all worked to undermine the credibility of the Vorster faction and of its strategies for white survival and prosperity.

The circumstances of Vorster's withdrawal from the premiership, his failure to engineer a quiet succession, and the extraordinary inability of the state to contain the information slush fund scandal which eventually brought this faction down in disgrace, are all still covered in mystery. While there is not enough evidence to show that his rivals engineered his downfall, rivals he assuredly had both within the party and in the state machinery itself and, at the very least, they did little to save him while they derived immense benefit from his fall.

External failure and sustained black urban revolt accompanied by a sharp drop in investors' confidence itself, in part, augmented by the Republic's external payments problems—the beginnings of the first serious recession since the Nationalists came to power—created a crisis of confidence among whites which had been variously characterized as a legitimation or a hegemonic crisis. The imperative task of the state, or whoever gained control of it, would be to restore confidence among whites and among investors abroad and to pacify the blacks in more lasting ways. In dealing with capital, the bargaining power of the state was less than it had been before even given the signs that some concessions on labor issues were already in the pipeline. Satisfying the capitalist class would be important in securing the confidence of foreign governments in the area of imperialist strategic cooperation in Africa also.

One area where the collaboration between the state and big business had grown importantly was that of Defense, but for reasons of Afrikaner historical sentiment, this had not been a central institutional area for personal power in the National Party. In any event, minded by the Cape Nationalist plutocrat, P.W. Botha, Defense had grown considerably in spending power and bureaucracy in the 1960s and 1970s. Overshadowed by civilian institutions of repression and intelligence yet beholden to its minister who not only responded to its interests but seemed to swallow its formulae for "survival," hook, line and sinker, it became a readily-available and potentially-formidable organizational base for a challenge to the Vorster faction and the planned succession of Mulder to the premiership.

It required no great perspicacity on Botha's part in contending for the leadership to seek the support of another disgruntled element in the white population, namely capital. This was in any event dictated by the economic crisis facing South Africa, but it was also strategically necessary—for securing the external Western endorsements of apartheid's struggle to survive. Ideologically, also, there was a basis for greater cooperation not only in the Cape Nationalists' greater "liberalism" but also in the fact that the armed forces' leadership had a necessarily greater "cosmopolitanism" than the civilian instruments of repression for various reasons: the imperial past, training experience abroad, especially before the arms embargo, the dependence on strategic doctrines based on globalist anticommunist counterinsurgency, and continuing contact with Israeli and other military leaders themselves inserted into the global imperialist military alliance system.[3] The policies that Botha proclaimed were an assemblage of concessions to business interests which were neither systematically thought out nor consistently implemented but which were to emerge hesitantly and fragmentarily in response to "crises." They signified an attempt to graft the commonplaces of counterinsurgency onto the structure of racist rule and ideology in a pretended "total strategy" whose most distinctive feature was precisely its lack of a strategic or political purpose beyond that of pushing back the threats to the ruling oligarchy. In execution even that lacked both coherence and conclusiveness.[4]

With regard to domestic politics, the significant point is that Botha was trying, with the aid of the military, to unite business and state behind an essentially military solution of South Africa's problem—in my view, the economic emphasis of this stance is easily overstated— with a promise of political reform. Reform, insofar as it was meant to imply the relaxation of racial discrimination and oppression, was made necessary both by the demonstrated failure of policies based on repression alone to curb and forestall black revolt, and by the increasing impracticality of running the economy along strict apartheid lines. But reform meant first and foremost manipulating divisions of race and of class among blacks in order to incorporate larger numbers of them both as cheap and abundant manpower and as, at best, privileged subalterns in the defense of white capitalist power. Here again the range of concessions to be made was not clear, reforms being extended reluctantly and episodically in response to "crises" produced by the failure of previous reforms.

Much has been said and written about the "total strategy" which Botha proclaimed and the substantial direct presence of the military in politics and in law and order maintenance functions which it brought about. In some ways, it represents a well-known tendency of armies to move into politics in times of hegemonic crisis. It is, however, more important as the effect of carrying politics into the state machinery itself which becomes factionalized, a process intimately related to the direct role played by the state in Afrikaner accumulation, and to the creation of the Afrikaner bureaucratic bourgeoisie. Its significance ultimately lies not in the capacity of the state to manage crises, "hegemonic" or otherwise, but in the lack of cohesion of the state of which it is a result.

The reforms that Botha has been compelled to concede range from the constitutional to the sexual and include most significantly labor laws and mobility laws, as well as the new doctrines of survival. They have not only produced the well-known splits within the white polity, but have fundamentally undermined the cogency of the ideology of the racist state and must force it to even greater eclecticism and opportunism both in its mobilizing slogans and in its blueprints for action. To an extent, that reflects the diversity of the elements that constitute the power bloc and their varying, often conflictual, hold on the state or various parts of it. None of this warrants the belief often voiced that the Botha program expressed the ascendancy of monopoly capital and the submission of the state to its needs. The state and those in the capitalist class who depend upon it still have need for their own defense, sometimes against the encroachments of those larger capitalist interests they have perforce to serve and with which they are in alliance.

While the reshufflings and the coalition politics have been going on within the state and the power bloc, mass struggles have also developed in response to the changing external circumstances and the internal crises of capitalism and racial domination. It will suffice for present purposes only to mention in a summary fashion the most significant points related to the policies of apartheid towards Africa.

In the 1960s, especially after 1964 when the state had all but destroyed the internal organizational base of the national movement, and in the early to mid-1970s, radical opponents of the regime generally expected a guerrilla struggle eventually to develop more or less along the lines of the struggles in the former Portuguese colonies and Zimbabwe, and for such a struggle to be closely led from the outside. There were many in 1976 who expected the liberation movements to march in and carry the struggle to victory. The success of the Frelimo stimulated great enthusiasm and high expectations, as would the defeat of South Africa and its allies in the Angolan Civil War, subsequently. In addition, or as a result, large numbers of militants found their way out of the country into the training camps of the ANC. Equally striking was the radicalizing effect of the success of Marxist movements: radical socialism became the ground on which the struggle was debated for an increasing number of students and workers.

Developments in the industrial and rural contexts reinforced working class militancy and radicalism, but now in a context in which there was a stronger impulse towards organization and the limited scope conceded by the state in part responding to international pressure. The remarkable growth in trade union organization and in working class community activity have also imposed radical socialism on the consciousness of the mass struggles.

Growing South African violence against neighboring countries, intended to force the expulsion of ANC activists from countries bordering on South Africa and to exclude SWAPO from southern Angola, have had perverse effects in that they have intensified the sense of being beleaguered and embattled among the domestic population in very much the same way that the escalation of aggression by Ian Smith's forces alienated the domestic population, driving the young into the armed struggle. Here, however, with the particular difficulties facing guerrilla infiltration and war, the popular response has taken the form of direct, many-sided resistance within the country. What is particularly noticeable is the series of attacks on collaborators reflecting a growing attitude of war, which is linked to the failure of the structures for collaboration like the Botha constitution and the Bantustans.

The use of collaboration strategies both in South Africa and in the neighboring countries, though it has produced deep division and bloody confrontations among the oppressed themselves, has, however, also provided ready "proxy" targets for the enraged masses and highlighted an area of weakness for the regime—its dependence on black manpower. The links between collaboration within South Africa in internal repression and the collaboration of certain groups and states across its borders are not lost upon the oppressed; rather, they contribute to a polarization and a radicalization that links repression in South Africa to the imperialist-aided aggressions of the South African state in neighboring countries.

Finally, the public and defiant avowal of support for the ANC in the mass actions of the last two years has represented a major setback for state policy intended to "externalize" and so marginalize the ANC. Since the 1970s many reformers of apartheid, both native and foreign, have dreamed of an internal settlement with some "moderate" alternative which would facilitate their stragety of assimilating the ANC (and SWAPO) to an external "communist danger" which it would be legitimate for Western states and well-disposed African states to assist South Africa in fighting. Undoubtedly the ANC has won "hearts and minds" by its own effort, but in launching war upon it, Botha identified it as the ultimate obstacle to the perpetuation of racist capitalism, however reformed.

For the state, the disposition of the domestic black population has become the principal obstacle to the success of its policies in Africa, policies designed in the first place to neutralize that population's revolutionary potential. Issuing from its internal politics, the foreign policy of South Africa continues to founder on those politics in ways that also hamper, as we shall presently show, the policies of Western states that are well-disposed towards it.

POLICIES TOWARDS AFRICA

Against the background of its domestic politics, it should be easier to see the African policy of the South African state clearly, its purpose and its irreconcilable contradictions. It should also be easier to see why this policy must necessarily be one of violence, intolerant of independent neighbors with radical socialist aspirations.

Faced with growing international isolation, Verwoerd conceived of the idea of a South African common market, based uon the former High Commission Territories then destined to become independent as Botswana, Lesotho, and Swaziland, but also capable of admitting other states further north. South Africa was confident of being able to hold on to the advantages which its system of communication, its mines, and its generally higher level of industrialization had given it. Economic and technical aid, of which emergent African states seemed always to be in need, was held out as a promised reward to those who would cooperate. Under Vorster, this policy was pursued more vigorously but with the emphasis on southern Africa tending to give way to a search for allies anywhere on the continent. In southern Africa the most important task of foreign policy was to assist the embattled white colonies and so draw them to a greater dependence on South Africa. The Cabora Bassa Dam Project and the Kunene River Scheme arose out of such attempts as did the support for the rebel British colony. While encroaching on Rhodesia's markets in southern Africa and elsewhere, Pretoria encouraged a rebellion which set back the economic development of Zimbabwe and the growth of Rhodesian capitalism by many years. Simultaneously, it was making definite encroachments on the economies of Portuguese colonies which before the wars of liberation had been all but closed to foreigners.

Encouraged by the attitude of Lesotho and Swaziland, and above all by Banda's collaboration, Vorster was to launch his policy of "dialogue" with the aid of France and the most francophile African heads of state, Houphouet-Boigny and Bongo. At this stage the predominant aim of policy was to break the solidarity of African states, to open markets, isolate the liberation movement, and gain wider international acceptance. Western states assigned Pretoria an important role in the region and in their naval strategies—quite apart from the considerable economic significance of South Africa, especially for Britain. That support is permanently recorded in United Nations documents where the West opposed every anti-apartheid initiative whether regarding South Africa itself or Namibia, or proffered in compromise diplomatic diversions and strategems that helped Pretoria more than its enemies— the ill-fated Western Contact Group being perhaps the most outstanding of these.

Although there were acts of aggression committed against neighboring states, particularly against Zambia, by South Africa and its Rhodesian ally, Pretoria's optimism about its prospects in Africa may have acted to moderate its use of force. There was a built-in ambiguity in the relationship with Zambia arising from a number of important considerations. Zambia employed white South Africans in mines owned or (later) managed by a South African multinational company. Thanks to UDI, trade between South Africa and Zambia was considerable. While the impact of guerrilla attacks on South Africa itself was small, Zambia's identification as a Western-leaning non-aligned state raised hopes about its own eventual "moderation" while giving it protection in so far as direct force against it would not have been well-received in the West. In addition, with the role of the military being subordinated to the all-important BOSS, the use of massive force did not readily suggest itself to the Vorster faction. Vorster preferred to use the instruments he personally controlled and the measures to which they lent themselves most readily. Finally, it was the assumption of state policy at the time that the decisive theater was the domestic one where great faith was placed in police repression while Pretoria blithely believed that it could separate the two spheres and forge gainful relations with African states without reference to South Africa's internal politics.

It was with the Angolan intervention that South African military coercion assumed an altogether different order of magnitude. Having been caught unprepared by the Portuguese coup and unable to formulate a response to Mozambican independence, South Africa was presented with an entirely different set of circumstances in the Angolan case. First, the South African military was on familiar terrain where it had been fighting SWAPO all along. Second, the division of the anticolonial forces into three movements, two of which had leaders that were strongly connected to the CIA in the case of FNLA and to both the CIA and the Portuguese military in the case of UNITA, provided tempting opportunity. American encouragement as well as indications of support from some African states led Vorster to believe that the action would produce a resounding success for his African and global diplomacy.[5] Finally, all the indications are that the military, and no doubt their defense minister, P.W. Botha, were eager to intervene, fearing the gain to SWAPO should the MPLA triumph and perhaps hoping to demonstrate to South Africa and the world their prowess with what they thought would be an easy victory. It is highly significant, however, that the action did not then involve a major military commitment to fight to a successful outcome or even to involve the South African public in this campaign.

In the recriminations that followed over the United States' failure to back the South African action, as Pretoria had evidently been led to expect that it would, Vorster revealed an old Afrikaner nationalist suspicion of the reliability of its Western allies. There would also occur some public acts of defiance by Vorster during the Carter period which would produce a marked deterioration in relations. Vorster, clearly, had not fully appreciated the evolving United States' role in Africa and the opportunities it might create for Pretoria.

Yet, Carter was weak and in the last two years of Vorster's premiership the Botha faction judged more accurately which way the wind was blowing in the United States and how much closer their own attitudes to both Angola and Namibia were to those of the dominant interests in the American ruling class. Attacks on Angola increased, attempts to revivify UNITA were stepped up, and with a murderous attack on SWAPO refugees in Cassinga, the military sought to overturn plans for a United Nations settlement of the Namibian problem with Angolan cooperation. When Botha took over in 1979 this aggression increased as did strikes by Rhodesia against Mozambique, Zambia, and on one occasion Angola too. While it is generally believed that South Africa recoiled from a negotiated international settlement of the Namibian issue because of the unexpected (by South Africa and the West) victory of ZANU in the Zimbabwean elections, it is difficult to see any evidence that suggests that the South African military were ever in favor of abandoning Namibia or allowing elections that might have even the remotest possibility of bringing SWAPO to power. Subsequently, Namibia would become more than ever their *chasse gardée* and a testing ground for their doctrines of counterinsurgency and for the use of ethnic armies and military men bequeathed by fascist Portugal and racist Rhodesia.

The thrust of South Africa's African policy under Botha was to be southern African rather than continent-wide, corresponding to the extent of effective applicability of South Africa's military power and, as luck would have it, coinciding with an American decision after Reagan's accession to give the highest priority to "fighting communism" in southern Africa while treating the rest of sub-saharan Africa as less important.

Botha sought to create a constellation of southern African states in elaboration of the idea initially raised by Verwoerd and pursued to some degree by Vorster. The only innovation under the new regime lay in the degree to which the state was disposed to use military force to coerce its neighbors out of any alternative arrangements they might devise, and the use of a variety of subversive forces to disrupt economic installations and especially those linking several countries, for example, the Mozambique-Zimbabwe pipeline and the Benguela railway line. Consolidating and expanding South African economic influence might be expected to appeal to the business class and was often seen as primarily reflecting the pressure on the state from this class. Yet it was for more important in hampering the development of independent links with the major capitalist countries. It was an attempt to force recognition of the intermediary subordinate-imperialist role that South Africa had always sought for itself, now in circumstances where it was quite feasible that some of these countries, notably Zimbabwe, might have strong attractions for international capital.

The African policy of Botha is linked to the "total strategy" proclaimed in the famous Defence White Papers and on various occasions by both Malan and Botha. Seeing South Africa as confronted with a total, communist-inspired onslaught, the state sought by a combination of "reform" at home to win hearts and minds, and decisive military action in the region. Premised on strong cooperation between the state and big capital, the strategy envisaged the encouragement of collaborating classes and strata among Blacks while also using racial and ethnic cleavages to divide and so weaken opposition. Nonessential racialist shibboleths would be swept aside while the targeting of internal repression would be more discriminating and less provocative. Frankel has shown the derivation of this notion from the strategic writings of General Beaufre which are treated as Holy Writ by the South African military.[6] What has been little stressed however is its vacuity which echoes the banalities and commonplaces of Beaufre's own conceptions—notions that have, as it happens, been used elsewhere without much success.

In its South African version, "total strategy" applies principally to the removal of the threat of insurgency from Namibia and South Africa itself. It contains no guidance to external policy beyond the militarization of diplomacy and the overkill that necessarily follows. It is nevertheless of greater ideological significance in so far as it made possible the translation of apartheid's parochial defense to a cosmopolitan global function in the defense of imperialism's peripheries. Its embrace and proclamation by the South African military was itself evidence of their self-identification with the wider counterinsurgency culture in the West. If the South African regime gained through this doctrine a plausible formula for survival that gave it more flexibility than more conventional apartheid doctrines allowed, it also sought to link its own concerns with those of international capital and specifically those of the United States.

Yet despite its portentousness and seeming adroitness the new approach was far from coherent or even clearly purposeful. Reference has already been made to its fragmentary and reactive concessions to reform in domestic politics. In Namibia as in South Africa it could not succeed for lack of a viable political purpose to which any "hearts and minds" that were at all human hearts and minds could be won. Often as applied to neighboring states, particularly in the earlier period, to Angola, Mozambique, and Zimbabwe, it amounted to little more than an unfocused destabilization and disruption leading to no clear benefit for South Africa. Even when aggression aimed to evict ANC cadres from neighboring countries, it threatened to incite sections of the local populations to militant identification with the ANC cause, thus spreading rather than containing the problem of "insurgency." Often it was conducted, as seems to be the case with the MNR and also with some of the raids into Botswana and Angola, by elements of the security forces subjected to no rational direction from the highest levels.

It was the United States policy toward Angola that was to give South African destabilization the global significance it needed and the real possibility to implicate imperialism more strongly and more dependably in the defense of the South African state. In a move that must have very few precedents in great power diplomacy outside the US-Israel relationship, Washington proceeded under Reagan to tie its own policy to that of South Africa in Namibia (though by necessary implication, in other areas as well) through the principle of "linkage."[7] Eager to eject the Cubans from Angola and to reverse the "Soviet victory" there, but lacking Congressional support and still constrained by the post-Vietnam syndrome, the Reagan administration found South Africa to be a useful military proxy in Angola. Others too were recruited or coordinated to help Savimbi and Botha: Morocco, Zaire, Saudi Arabia, and France under Giscard D'Estaing (helping FLEC and Mobutu) and less directly Senegal under the Negritude poet and philosopher Leopold Senghor, and Ivory Coast.

Thanks to the United States' "linkage" politics, South Africa felt less pressured to agree to an international settlement of the Namibian dispute but instead stepped up its attacks on Angola and neighboring countries generally and, from 1981, actually reoccupying Angolan territory. In this way it was also able to block any possibility of an improvement of relations between the United States and Angola, thus turning "linkage" to its own good use.

The destablization of Mozambique was also an international effort with South Africa playing the central role in the effort to roll back the frontiers of socialism. When Botha felt the need for a diplomatic approach in 1984, forcing upon its eastern neighbor a leonine pact, the Nkomati Accords, the security and military forces continued the destabilization to the extent that subsequently the state was either unable to halt it (in accordance with its promises to Maputo) or judged it safest for its own cohesion to abandon the idea of calling a halt to destabilization. Although Nkomati was welcomed as a signal victory in the Western capitals, there were evidently many who looked forward to a complete reversal of the Frelimo government or, at the very least, a dramatic showdown with the USSR comparable to Sadat's repudiation of Moscow in 1973. When that did not happen, little or nothing was done to ease the pressure of subversion against Mozambique.

South Africa achieved for itself a military role in United States policy in southern Africa which would enable it not only to secure a stronger commitment of Western support for its own internal defense and "reform," but would give it something of a veto on Western policy. Attacks on the smaller countries, while determined by more local concerns—driving out the ANC and demonstrating strength to anxious white supporters—have also indicated the comparative lack of Western interest in restraining Pretoria or the certain knowledge on its part that Western disapproval in these cases is far outweighed by approval of the larger role and by the attractions of South Africa itself, especially for Britain and the United States.

By contrast, however, having begun with a distinctly hostile attitude, South African policy towards Zimbabwe has been much more restrained than that applied to other states of socialist aspiration. Commercial considerations here are important as they once were in the case of Zambia. The absence of a "Soviet factor" and Zimbabwe's more limited involvement in the South African struggle have also been noted. But, essentially, United States and British interest in the country has been sufficient to hold back Pretoria which can content itself with simply blocking Harare's every attempt towards independent economic development that would disengage it from the South African communications system and economy, or that could make it a rival attraction for foreign capital.

While South African policy has been distinctly less concerned with the rest of Africa in recent years, developments there have clearly aided South Africa in its southern African policies and in forging the new relationship with imperialism on the continent. The divisions in the OAU, the economic and ecological crises, and the virtual collapse of Nigeria's economic position (and for a time its nationalist commitments on the continent), all made the United States' and South Africa's passage much smoother. Weakened by the international recession and their own reactions to it and by a deepening external dependence, most African states are simply not disposed or able to threaten credible sanctions against those who collaborate with Pretoria. The truly radical states are, in most cases, among the poorest and often subject to severe military pressures on their own ground.

Yet, there have emerged significant openings for Pretoria—in the neocolonial semi-military alliances that are emerging under United States auspices, through the activities of multinationals (the oil swaps which provoked strong reaction in Nigeria in the late 1970s, for example), through undeclared trade and informal deals, and through the informal, quasi-non-governmental activities of right-wing pressure groups (those associated with the Reverend Moon being perhaps the most colorful). The abortive attempt to overthrows the Seychelles government, supposedly without the authorization of Pretoria, indicated the disposition of the South African state machinery to intervene forcefully outside the southern African area. The failure of total strategy at home and in the immediate vicinity may yet provoke diversionary actions further afield, while growing anti-apartheid agitation in the West may create the need for Pretoria to do even more to prove its worth to imperialism, pulling American chestnuts out of fires further to the north.

What remains as certain fact is the need for South Africa to retain southern Africa as its distinctive sphere of influence and to disrupt attempts by its key states to forge independent economic and military links. To that extent, attempts to revive a progressive African unity or to orient southern African economies more to the north in order to escape South African satellitization—to use the interior language of the Cold War—will always be resisted by South Africa.

For the rest, the military element has become central to South African diplomacy and this now appears irreversible. While there are important battles still to be fought at the diplomatic level, African states will increasingly have to look to their own defenses, individual and collective, or succumb. That however raises the problem of external military assistance which is linked to the equally delicate issue of the balance of power among states more important than South Africa in regard to the continent. Such considerations would take us too far from our present task, yet that is where this reflection seems to lead irresistibly. In any event, whatever the level at which they may feel able to resist South Africa or even a "reformed" South African sub-imperialism, these states can have no greater source of strength than their own people without whose committed, democratic engagement in anti-imperialist struggles in their own "independent" countries the opposition to South Africa and those it serves can only be feeble.

NOTES

1.   See also H. Adam and H. Giliomee, *Ethnic Power Mobilized: Can South Africa Change?* New Haven: Yale University Press, 1979.
2.   See also Dan O'Meara, *Volkskapitalisme: Class, Capital, and Ideology in the*

Development of Afrikaner Nationalism, 1934–1948, Cambridge: Cambridge University Press, 1983.

3. P. Frankel, *Pretoria's Praetorians: Civil-Military Relations in South Africa* (Cambridge: Cambridge University Press, 1984) deals with some of these issues.

4. R. Davies and P. O'Meara, "Total Strategy in Southern Africa" in *Journal of Southern African Studies* (1985).

5. D. Geldenhuys, *The Diplomacy of Isolation: South African Foreign Policy Making,* New York: St. Martin's Press, 1984.

6. Frankel, *op cit., passim.*

7. See G. Bender, J.S. Coleman and R. Sklar (eds), *African Crisis Areas and United States Foreign Policy,* Berkeley: University of California Press, 1985.

Index

Cuba, 118, 157
Cuban, 121, 129
Cuban troops, 131
Cultural subordination, 140
Customs Tariff Commission, 40

Daniels, Romero, 68
Darwinism, 58
Davidson, 9, 21
Davis,Robert, 21
De Beers, 58, 73
Defiance Campaign, 153
Department of Mining and Taxation, 41
Dependent capitalism, 124
de Saussure, 6
Destabilization, ii, iii
Diamonds, 16, 57, 68
Dispossession, 3, 5
Domestic service, 146, 150
Domestic Workers Association, 146
Domestic Workers and Employers Project, 146
Dominent aristocracy, 10
Domination, 24
Dominican Republic, 118
Drought Investigation Committee, 40
Du Bois, 8
Dutch, 5, 53, 56, 57
Dutch East India Company, 3
Dutt, Palme R., 56, 57

East Indian, 55
Economic domination,
Economic exploitation, 15, 63
Economic nationalism, 39, 42, 45
Economic sanctions, ii
Egypt, 119
Engels, F., 9, 66, 91, 92, 100
England, 8
English proletariat, 66
English settler, 60
English speaking farmers-natal, 36
Ethnicity, 6, 18
Ethno-nationalist party, 165
Europe, 120
European, "Enlightenment," 94

White colonialism, 26, 121
White dominance, 5, 100
White Hall, 95
White House, 130
White man's country, 5, 64
White minority, 1, 2, 5, 8, 14, 17, 30, 95
White nurses, 150, 1
White polity, 167
White population, 161, 166
White race, 4, 11
White ruling class, 96
White settlers, 3, 6, 10, 14, 17, 31, 64, 106, 107, 112
White settler state, 8, 112
White states, 124
White supremacy, 6, 7, 67, 145
White unity, 164
White working class, 7, 38, 40, 46, 109
White workers Chauvinism, 38
Whites, 5, 11, 52, 107
Wilmont, Alexander, 62, 84
Wizner, Frank, 113
Wolpe, Harold, ii, 138
Women oppression, 14, 137, 140
Women question, 137, 138, 139
World Bank, 117
World Congress of League Against Imperialism, 137, 138, 169
World economy, 16
World War I, 95, 101, 106
World War II, 97, 115, 118

Xhosa, 28, 29, 54

Youth League Manifesto, 99

ZANU, iii
ZAPU, iii
Zambia, 170
Zimbabwe, iii, 2, 19, 30, 31, 46, 48, 80, 112, 113, 121, 126, 129, 130, 156, 161, 170
Zimmerwaldists, 103
Zulu, 29, 54
Zulu women, 156